Scientist, Soldier,
Statesman, Spy

COUNT RUMFORD

The Extraordinary Life of a Scientific Genius

G.I. BROWN

Foreword by
Susan Greenfield

SUTTON PUBLISHING

First published in the United Kingdom in 1999 by
Sutton Publishing Limited · Phoenix Mill
Thrupp · Stroud · Gloucestershire · GL5 2BU

Paperback edition first published in 2001

British Library Cataloguing in Publication Data
A catalogue record for this book is available from the British Library

ISBN 0-7509-2674-0

Typeset in 13/16pt Perpetua.
Typesetting and origination by
Sutton Publishing Limited.
Printed in Great Britain by
J.H. Haynes & Co., Ltd, Sparkford.

CONTENTS

Foreword *by Susan Greenfield*   v

Preface   vii

Acknowledgements   viii

1   An Eye for the Main Chance   1

2   Fortunes of War   19

3   Bavarian Adventure   37

4   The Countess   60

5   The Nature of Heat   77

6   The Ingenious Inventor   95

7   The Royal Institution   114

8   A Female Dragon   137

9   Final Verdict   159

Appendices:

   1: The first page of Rumford's spy letter   163

   2: The first page of Rumford's 'Miscellanius

     Observations upon the State of the Rebel Army'   165

   3: Rumford's Essays   166

Notes   168

Bibliography   173

Index   176

For Barbara, Helen and Louise

FOREWORD

B enjamin Thompson, Count Rumford of the Holy Roman Empire, has always enjoyed a mixed press. President Roosevelt ranked Rumford, along with Benjamin Franklin and Thomas Jefferson, as 'the greatest mind America has produced', while a more recent commentator has written that 'he was unbelievably cold-blooded, inherently egotistic and a snob'. Of course these two assessments are not mutually exclusive and this very readable biography of Thompson explores his complex personality. In his scientific work Thompson played a major role in establishing both the Royal Institution and the theory that heat was a mode of motion. Both the Institution and the theory continue to exert their influence to this day.

Thompson's notoriety stemmed from the necessity of making a living in a time of drastic political upheaval and he thus had to trim his sails accordingly. In this he was no worse than the French mathematician Pierre-Simon Laplace who at least avoided the guillotine, unlike his colleague the chemist Antoine Lavoisier, whose widow Thompson later married and lived unhappily ever after. Thompson's womanizing (he left at least two illegitimate children) was not particularly at odds with the social mores of the upper classes at the time. To appreciate this one has only to think of the activities of the Prince Regent, Lord Nelson and Lord Palmerston (Lady Palmerston being one of Rumford's mistresses for a while). In Thompson's case, and perhaps the others as well, the cause of such patterns of behaviour was the interminable wars which were fought in the late eighteenth and early nineteenth centuries. For most of his adult life Thompson was an officer in one army or another in America and Europe. He fought against the rebels in the American War of Independence and later helped Bavaria to retain its independence during the wars against France. In all of this Thompson's actions increasingly reflected the *sturm-und-drang* atmosphere of the period as the war continued seemingly without end; indeed Thompson died the year before the Battle of Waterloo finally put an end to the conflict.

Why Thompson is singled out for criticism, in a way that some of the others mentioned above are not, is because he did scientific work. Scientists are, in the popular imagination, supposed to be a special type of person above the conflicts of the world. This image was constructed during the eighteenth century and still exerts a powerful influence today. George Brown, in this splendid biography, shows that science is a very human activity which can be undertaken even in the most extreme of circumstances.

Susan Greenfield
Director, Royal Institution of Great Britain
July 1999

PREFACE

Count Rumford was largely responsible for the founding of the Royal Institution of Great Britain two hundred years ago, and I have taken the opportunity of its bicentenary to re-tell the remarkable story of his life.

Born Benjamin Thompson into a humble farming family in Massachusetts in 1753, he built up during his lifetime an international reputation as a soldier, statesman, scientist, inventor and social reformer in America, England, Bavaria and France. He was a colonel in the British Army; was elected a member of the Royal Society in England in 1779; was knighted by King George III in 1781; and was made a Count of the Holy Roman Empire by the Elector of Bavaria in 1792.

Yet he died and was buried, almost alone, in Paris in 1814, and very few people today have ever heard of him. This book describes his very real achievements, which placed him well ahead of his time as someone who tried to apply scientific methods to improve living standards, particularly the lot of the poor, and concludes that he has been forgotten not because of what he did but because of the way in which he did it.

ACKNOWLEDGEMENTS

Rumford was a prolific writer and correspondent and he left behind much of his work. His eighteen Essays, listed in Appendix 3, were published in England in his lifetime, and much other material has survived. It is, however, very widely spread with much of it in the possession of such institutions as the Royal Society, the Royal Institution, the Public Record Office, and Birmingham University in England; and Harvard University, Michigan University, the Massachusetts Historical Society, Dartmouth College and the American Academy of Arts and Science in the United States. Some letters are owned privately.

His life has been studied and recorded by three main researchers – the Americans the Revd G.E. Ellis and Sanborn C. Brown, and the Englishman W.J. Sparrow – and I acknowledge the debt that I owe to their work. I have made particular use of the four volumes of Rumford's 18 Essays; of Ellis's 1871 *Memoir*; of *The Complete Works of Count Rumford* published in 1874 by The American Society of Arts and Sciences in Boston, and by Macmillan & Co. in 1876 in England; and of *The Collected Works of Count Rumford*, edited by Sanborn C. Brown and published in America in 1970–1. Other books and articles I have consulted are listed in the Bibliography.

Acknowledgements

I am grateful to the Librarians at the Royal Society and at Eton College for their help; to Professor Susan Greenfield for her Foreword; to Dr Frank A.J.L. James, the Reader in History of Science at the Royal Institution, for his helpful comments; to the William L. Clements Library in the University of Michigan, the Deutsches Museum in Munich, Karin and Colin Oakley, Christiane Morin and Neil Shearer for providing illustrations; and to Peter Harper for drawing the maps and most of the line diagrams. I would also like to thank my wife for her constant support and for her many helpful suggestions.

The statue of Count Rumford in Maximilianstrasse, Munich.

AN EYE FOR THE MAIN CHANCE

Famous men are generally afforded grand funerals, but it was not so for Count Rumford. He was buried on 24 August 1814 in the cemetery at Auteuil, on the outskirts of Paris, in the presence of just a few friends and neither his ex-wife, the former Mme Lavoisier, nor his daughter was there. The inscription on his tombstone summarized his life's work with the words: 'The celebrated physicist and enlightened philanthropist, whose discoveries in light and heat made his name illustrious, and whose work to better the lot of the poor will always be cherished by humanity.' But there was no reference to the complex nature of Rumford's character, and it was only when that came to light after his death that it was possible to understand why his funeral had been such a solitary affair, and why his name and his great achievements are not well known today.

He was born Benjamin Thompson, on 26 March 1753 in Woburn, a small rural town in Massachusetts in north-east America. This state had been founded as an English colony when the Pilgrim Fathers, sailing in the *Mayflower*, landed on the shores of the Bay of Cape Cod, at what is now New Plymouth, in December 1620. One of Benjamin's paternal ancestors, James Thompson, had landed ten years later,

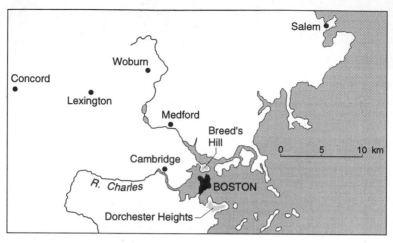

The area around Boston in 1770.

along with John Winthrop who subsequently became the first Governor of Massachusetts.

Benjamin's father ran the small family farm that had been set up by his grandfather, and his mother was the daughter of an army officer who had served with distinction in the long war against the French and the Indians. Benjamin was their first child. In the normal course of events the farm would have passed to him when he grew up and he would have spent his life as a husbandman, but fate intervened when his father died, aged just twenty-six, when Benjamin was only twenty months old. The farm was then taken over by his uncle Hiram and, when Benjamin was three years old, his mother married another farmer, Josiah Pierce, and had four more children. Later in life, Benjamin told a Swiss friend, Professor M.A. Pictet, that his father's death 'was a circumstance purely accidental, which, while I was still an infant, decided my destiny'.[1] He went on, 'I was obliged to form the habit of thinking and acting for myself, and of depending on my own for a livelihood.'[2]

It is not easy to decide where the truth lies regarding his subsequent upbringing. On the one hand, Benjamin wrote to Pictet in 1797 that 'recollection of the happy scenes of my infancy and early youth is inexpressibly interesting and dear to me'.[3] Yet a little later, he was telling the same friend that he had never liked his stepfather, describing him as a 'tyrannical'[4] husband. He also said that he had resented his mother's re-marrying and did not like her rearing a large family. It is, however, most likely that these later views were simply an attempt by Benjamin to romanticize his image as a self-made man and, as he commonly did throughout his life, to present events in what he decided was the most favourable light at any particular moment.

All the evidence suggests that he was well treated in his early years. He was left about 50 acres of woods and farmland in his father's will, and his grandfather instructed his uncle Hiram to pay him 16 shillings a year until he was fourteen years old and to support his mother while she remained a widow.

He was also given a better education than any of his siblings, going to the local school in Woburn, and then to schools in Byfield and Medford. It is said that 'he exhibited an intense mental activity, a spirit of ingenuity and inventiveness, and was found seeking for amusement in things which afterwards proved to lead him to the profitable and beneficiary occupations of his mature life. He showed a particular ardour for arithmetic and mathematics, and it was remembered of him, afterwards, that his playtime, and some of his proper worktime, had been given to ingenious mechanical contrivances, soon leading to a curious interest in the principles of mechanics and natural philosophy'.[5] But though he was a bright student at school, his friends reported that he was very uncooperative at home when he was required to help on the farm.

On leaving school, aged thirteen, he was apprenticed to, and lived with, John Appleton of Salem, who ran a large general store. Later, aged sixteen, he worked for Hopestill Capen, a Boston trader. It soon became clear, however, that he was not a natural shop assistant. Indeed, Mr Capen wrote to his mother that he 'oftener found her son under the counter with gimlets, knife and saw constructing some little machine, or looking over some book of science, than behind it arranging the cloths or waiting on customers'.[6] So it was not surprising that Mr Capen dispensed with his services in 1770, and Benjamin returned home.

A notebook that he kept between the ages of sixteen and nineteen confirms that he did not regard retailing very highly, while an early entry – 'never allow an opportunity of advancement to escape me'[7] – was to be one of the guiding lights of his life as he began the process of self-advancement not uncommon in ambitious young men with innate ability and plenty of energy. Somewhat later, he wrote that 'my thirst for knowledge became inextinguishable'[8] and he turned to some local friends for enlightenment.

A drawing by Thompson from a note-book he kept between 1769 and 1772. It is entitled 'A Council of State' and seems to include ten male heads, two female heads and a jackass.

Loammi Baldwin had the greatest influence. He lived across the road from Benjamin and, though he was nine years older, they struck up a lifelong friendship. Loammi was studying engineering so they had similar interests and their mutual passion for self-education led to long discussions and correspondence on a wide range of topics. At the same time the Revd Thomas Barnard, the minister at the Free Church at Salem, taught him mathematics and Dr Hay, the Woburn physician, took him in as a medical apprentice. Benjamin also found time to attend some lectures on experimental philosophy by Professor John Winthrop at what was then Harvard College in Cambridge; he began to learn French and fencing at a local private school; he had a great interest in music and played the violin; and he was an excellent draughtsman with very neat handwriting.

Entries in his notebook show, however, that his main interest was in science and technology; that he liked both the theoretical and the practical parts; and that he was talented. Before the age of fourteen he was able to calculate and trace the elements of a solar eclipse. He and Loammi tried to repeat Benjamin Franklin's experiment of flying a kite during a thunderstorm, only to find that they were engulfed in a flashing flame and, in Loammi's words, 'felt a general weakness in their joints and limbs and a kind of lifeless feeling'.[9] He built a supposed perpetual motion machine which he described as a combination of 'wheels and mechanical power', but Loammi reported that it 'was never possible to gain any information concerning the principles upon which it was expected to act'.[10] He built an electrical machine, not unlike today's Van de Graaf generator. Dr Hay found him one day operating on a pig to remove its windpipe. And he almost blew himself up while making some fireworks, commenting later that 'the force of gunpowder is so great, and its effects so sudden and so terrible, that, notwithstanding all the precautions possible, there is ever a considerable degree of danger attending the management of it, as I have more than once found to my cost'.[11]

The tenacity with which he approached this process of self-education is clearly shown by the rigid timetable he set himself when, at the age of seventeen, he was studying with

Dr Hay. On Mondays and Tuesdays he would study anatomy; on Wednesdays, physics; on Thursdays, surgery: on Fridays, chemistry; and on Saturdays, physics and surgery. On a typical day he would rise at 6 a.m., wash, and then exercise for the first hour and study for the second one. From 8 to 10, he had breakfast and attended prayers; and from 10 to 12, he studied. After lunch at 12, there was more full-time study until 4, when he relieved his mind by diversion or exercise for an hour. From 5 p.m. until bedtime at 11, he followed wherever his inclination led him. Such a rigorous timetable provides an early example of Thompson's passion for order and organization which he carried with him throughout his life.

His determination was very praiseworthy but it yielded no immediate financial support and the only money he had came from selling firewood which he chopped from the trees on the woodland he had inherited. So it was that, when he was eighteen, Benjamin decided to turn his hand to teaching, thinking that he could combine this with his studies. It was typical of the lucky breaks that spanned his career.

He began by boarding with local rich families so that he could teach their children reading, writing, arithmetic and some elementary science. He must have created a good impression because within a year he was invited by the Revd Timothy Walker, a minister at Concord in New Hampshire, to move there and run a school with 106 scholars. Concord had previously been called Rumford, after Romford, the English town in Essex, where its settlers had originated, but it had been renamed following a boundary change. Benjamin accepted the challenge and the move was typical of his whole life. His determination never to allow an opportunity to escape him was linked with an uncanny knack of always being in the right place at the right time.

The Revd Walker, who had been born in Woburn, was wealthy and had for years been a dominant local figure in Concord. He lived in a large house and owned three slaves. His daughter Sarah had married another Concord worthy, Colonel Benjamin Pierce, when he was sixty-three and she was thirty. Within a year, her husband had died, and she was left as the richest widow in Concord, with their son Paul.

When Benjamin first met her she had been widowed for only a few months, and he was a handsome nineteen-year-old, almost 1.8 metres tall, with carefully powdered auburn hair and blue eyes. He radiated self-confidence, had a twinkle in his eye, a polished, if somewhat haughty, manner, and an ability to talk knowingly on almost any topic.

In November 1772, within four months of their first meeting, they were married and Benjamin was changed from an impecunious, studious schoolmaster into a wealthy country gentleman with a large farm to run. He might, he said later, 'have been poor and unhappy all my life, if a woman had not loved me, if she had not given me a subsistence, a home and an independent fortune'.[12] His wife took him to Boston, 100 kilometres away, in a two-horse curricle, to be fitted with a Hussar cloak faced with scarlet shalloon, with mock-spangled buttons, and to have his hair done. Then she began the process of integrating him into her circle of friends, which Benjamin did not find at all distasteful.

A visit to a military review of the 2nd Provincial Regiment of New Hampshire on 13 November 1772 was typical. The Governor of New Hampshire, John Wentworth, who was taking the salute, was a relative of Mrs Thompson and her new husband jumped at the opportunity to make his presence felt. Mounted on a white horse and wearing his scarlet Hussar cloak, he created such an impression that he was quickly drawn into the governor's circle of friends. So much so that, when he was only twenty, the Governor offered him a major's commission in the 2nd New Hampshire Regiment. Few men can have had such sudden and meteoric promotion based on so little military background.

It was a propitious start to married life for Mr and Mrs Thompson and, despite their age difference, all seemed to be going smoothly when their daughter Sarah, commonly known as Sally, was born in October 1774. But later in life Benjamin used to say that 'she married me, not I her',[13] and it will never be known how the marriage might have developed had it not been cut short by political events culminating in the American War of Independence.

The war came about following a gradual breakdown in order in some of the colonies because they resented the way they were being treated by the British Government. In particular, they wanted to be freed from British taxation and to be allowed to run their own affairs, but that was frowned

The thirteen colonies in north-east America in 1770.

on in London. The Earl of Chatham, previously the elder William Pitt, wrote that 'The Americans must be subordinate. . . . They are children. They must obey, and we prescribe.'[14] And the Prime Minister Lord North, who was described by Dr Johnson as 'a man who fills a chair with a mind as narrow as the neck of a vinegar-cruet',[15] took a firm line.

A number of high-profile incidents heightened the tension. In March 1765 George Grenville, the then British

Prime Minister, introduced a Stamp Act imposing a tax on the sale of stamps, which had to be used on almost all printed matter. The resulting riots meant that the Act had to be repealed almost a year later and Grenville resigned. In 1770 a mob of sixty youths in Boston pelted a party of British soldiers with snowballs; in the resulting fracas, which came to be known as the Boston Massacre, three of the youths were shot dead by the army. In 1773 a tax imposed on tea led a group of Massachusetts citizens, disguised as North American Indians, to board three ships that were docked in Boston harbour. They ransacked the cargo – 298 chests of tea – and tipped it into the sea in what became known as the Boston Tea Party.

The British Government responded by closing the port of Boston to all traffic and announcing that Salem would henceforth be the capital of Massachusetts. They also passed a series of Acts called the Coercive or Intolerable Acts by the Americans, which, among other measures, forced Boston citizens to board British soldiers in their homes. In response, the First Continental Congress, at which all the colonies except Georgia were represented, was held in Philadelphia in September 1774, and called for the Acts to be repealed and for more civil disobedience to thwart the British. It also recommended the build-up of volunteer militia forces, known as Minutemen because they were supposed to be available at a minute's notice.

The area around Boston was the centre of opposition to British rule and the war broke out here on 19 April 1775 when a detachment of British troops, intent on capturing some of the colonists' military supplies, came under fire from local militiamen at Lexington and Concord to the north-west of Boston. In the fighting that followed, the British suffered 273 casualties, the Americans 93. The incident was immortalized in Longfellow's poem describing the ride of Paul Revere, a Boston silversmith, through the night of 18 April, to warn the local militiamen of the approach of the British Army:

> Listen my children, and you shall hear
> Of the midnight ride of Paul Revere . . .
>
> You know the rest. In the books you have read
> How the British Regulars fired and fled,
> How the farmers gave them ball for ball,
> From behind each fence and farmyard wall,
> Chasing the red-coats down the lane,
> Then crossing the fields to emerge again
> Under the trees at the turn of the road,
> And only pausing to fire and load.

Thomas Gage, the Governor of Massachusetts, commanded the soldiers in the British Army, and George Washington was appointed to organize and lead a new American Continental Army at the Second Continental Congress held at Philadelphia on 10 May 1775. A 43-year-old wealthy landowner and a colonel in the Virginia Militia, Washington volunteered to serve without pay and he set about organizing what he referred to as a 'mixed multitude'.[16]

'I am now Imbarked on a wide Ocean, boundless in its prospect,' he wrote, 'and from whence, perhaps, no safe harbour is to be found.'[17]

One of his first objectives was to force the British troops out of Boston, which was notoriously difficult to defend as it was dominated by high ground both to the north and to the south. His first attempt, involving the occupation of the high ground to the north at Breed's Hill, failed when he was defeated in what came to be known as the battle of Bunker Hill on 17 June 1775. The British victory was, however, very costly with 226 dead and 828 wounded (over 40 per cent of the troops involved), compared with American losses of 140 dead and 271 wounded.

Washington had more success when he occupied the high ground to the south at Dorchester on the night of 4/5 March 1776. By now his force was equipped with fifty-nine cannon that had been captured from the British base at Fort Ticonderoga on Lake Champlain and dragged on ox-drawn sledges over the winter snow all the way to Boston, some 300 kilometres distant. Both the city of Boston and the naval movements around it were so heavily threatened by this force that Gage decided to withdraw to fight again another day. And so, on 17 March, Washington was able to announce to Congress that 'it is with great pleasure I inform you that, about 9 o'clock in the forenoon, the Ministerial Army evacuated the Town of Boston'.[18]

Before and during the War of Independence the colonists had to decide which side to back. About one-third of them were against the British, and about one-third for, with the rest neutral. Even friends chose differently. Benjamin Thompson, for instance, accepted Governor Wentworth's offer of a British commission, while Loammi Baldwin became a major and later a colonel in Washington's army.

Thompson's choice pleased no one. The seasoned British officers in the 2nd New Hampshire Regiment resented having a man with no military experience thrust upon them. Many of the people of Concord and Woburn began to regard him as a traitor, and their viewpoint was reinforced when they discovered that Benjamin had employed two British deserters on his estate before sending them to General Gage in Boston with a request for clemency. As a result, the People's Committee of Concord summoned him to appear before them in December 1774 to answer a charge of 'being unfriendly to the cause of Liberty'.[19] The verdict of 'not proven' rather than 'not guilty' did not appease his accusers and he had to talk his way out of a second trial which took place on 18 May 1775.

The atmosphere remained distinctly hostile and by December, fearing a mob attack on his home, Thompson decided that it would be wise to leave the district. He wrote to his father-in-law: 'I thought it absolutely necessary to abscond for a while and seek a friendly asylum in some distant part. Fear of miscarriage prevents my giving a more particular account of this affair: but this you may rely upon, that I never did, nor ever will do, any action that may have the most distant tendency to injure the true interest of this my native country.'[20]

He sold some of his land to Loammi Baldwin's elder brother to raise some funds and on 13 October 1775 he was driven by his stepbrother to Narragansett Bay, some 80 kilometres south of Boston. His departure must have been organized in consultation with the British commanders because he was picked up by the frigate *Scarborough* and taken to Boston. He offered his services to General William Howe, who had just replaced General Gage as commander-in-chief, with a fulsome assurance of his loyalty to King George III.

Thompson lived in lodgings not far from Mr Capen's shop where he had worked five years earlier, and he was employed, under the control of Colonel Stephen Kemble, General Gage's brother-in-law, in collecting intelligence information about the rebels. He combined business with pleasure by having an affair with the wife of the editor of a revolutionary newspaper, *The Massachusetts Spy*, in the hope that he could persuade her to divulge the views of her husband's cronies.

But all that came to an end when the British evacuated Boston on 17 March 1776. Thompson was one of the ten thousand soldiers and civilians to leave and he made his way to England. He left his wife and daughter behind, having written to his father-in-law beseeching him to 'take kind care of my distressed family, and to take any opportunity to alleviate their trouble'.[21] He never saw his wife again and made no enquiries about her until some thirty years later when he wanted to remarry, and he had to wait for twenty years to see his daughter again.

Thompson's collecting of intelligence during his stay in Boston was simply an extension of the spying activities which he had been carrying out for some time. It has always seemed rather odd that Governor Wentworth offered him a commission in the British Army so readily. Perhaps it was on the agreement that he would act as a secret agent. The British were certainly anxious to limit the number of their deserters, and particularly keen to avoid them being recruited by the enemy. They also knew very little about the recently recruited American militia.

There is no doubt that General Gage and General Howe did receive letters containing sensitive military information, and many of them are still stored in the Public Record Office in London and in the William L. Clements Library in the University of Michigan. They are written in several different hands but one particularly long and informative one from Woburn, dated 6 May 1775, is in Benjamin Thompson's

Loammi Baldwin at the age of thirty, when he was a major in the American army.

handwriting. It claims to be based on information provided by Loammi Baldwin, a major in Washington's army, and by Dr Benjamin Church, the army's Surgeon-General. Dr Church was one of the most notorious wartime informers: he needed the money it provided to maintain both his high standard of living and his expensive mistress. But he was eventually arrested when the mistress, whom he used as a courier, delivered a message into the wrong hands. After being found guilty he was jailed and then, in 1777, transported into exile in the West Indies.

Thompson's letter gave important details of the planned attack on Boston, but what is of most interest today is the fact that much of it was originally written in invisible ink. This came to light in the 1950s when Professor Sanborn C. Brown and Mr Elbridge W. Stein subjected the letter to a thorough forensic examination. The short covering note had been written in Indian ink, but the large spaces between the lines had been filled with about 700 words written in a solution of gallotannic acid which, when dry, were invisible. They had subsequently been brought to light by soaking the letter in a solution of iron sulphate, which reacts with the acid to form iron gallotannate which is black. A solution of gallotannic acid can be made by soaking nutgalls, which are very common in Massachusetts, in water. At about the time the letter was being written, Thompson was complaining of suffering from diarrhoea, for which an infusion of nutgalls was a common remedy; this might have been used as a cover for his activities.

Brown and Stein further showed that the script of this letter matched that of Thompson's other letters and that the sealing wax matched that used by him elsewhere; moreover, the letter contained one of his common spelling errors – 'oppertunity' for opportunity.

The letter is not signed, but there can be little doubt that this early example of relatively sophisticated espionage was perpetrated by Thompson. Yet a few days after he wrote the letter, during his second trial, he claimed, 'I have done nothing contrary to the best interest of my country.'[22] But which country did he mean?

A further, less covert, example of his spying is found in an eleven-page report dated 4 November 1775 and signed 'B.T.' It was entitled 'Miscellanius Observations upon the State of the Rebel Army' and it was presented to General Howe shortly after Thompson arrived in Boston. The report was very comprehensive. It gave details of stores and equipment; artillery and small arms; powder and shot; the army command structure; clothing, feeding and general living conditions; health and medical facilities; and training methods and discipline. Overall, it presented a picture of an army with an estimated strength of about 15,000, ready to take the field. But the report was critical in some respects. The rebel riflemen, it said, were poor marksmen, the soldiers did not respect the authority of their officers because of 'the doctrine of independence and levellism that has been so effectively sown throughout the Country',[23] and 'the Army in general is not only very badly accoutered but is wretchedly cloathed and as dirty a set of mortals as ever disgraced the name of a Soldier'.[24]

Perhaps appearance doesn't matter. They did, after all, win the war, even if it took them eight years to do so.

FORTUNES OF WAR

The London in which Thompson found himself in April 1776 was not as it is today. Although it was the largest city in Europe, it had a population of only about 800,000 and it occupied a strip of land, 1.5 to 3 kilometres deep, north of the River Thames running from Hyde Park in the west to Wapping in the east. There was only a small area of buildings south of the river around Southwark and Rotherhithe.

The city was a hotbed of activity. So much so, that Samuel Johnson wrote that 'when a man is tired of London he is tired of life; for there is in London all that life can afford'.[1] And that was probably true enough for those who could afford it. Literature was fostered by Horace Walpole, James Boswell, William Cowper, Richard Sheridan and Edward Gibbon; art by Sir Joshua Reynolds, Thomas Gainsborough, John Zoffany, John Flaxman and Benjamin West; the theatre by John Kemble and Sarah Siddons; craftsmanship by Josiah Wedgwood and Thomas Sheraton; and gossip and scandal by the gentlemen's clubs, such as Whites, Boodles, Brooks and Crockfords, which evolved out of the earlier, and less cliquey, coffee-houses.

Yet behind the elegant façade associated with such high living there was a counter-balancing low life which involved

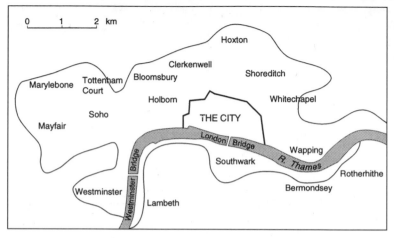

The built-up area of London around 1775.

squalor, suffering and inhumanity. Things might have been slightly better than earlier in the century but there was still far too much prostitution and drunkenness, too many unwholesome pastimes such as bare-fist boxing, cock-fighting and bull-baiting, and too many boy chimney sweeps, tramps, women cinder-sifters, rag-pickers and beggars. Much of this led to petty, and not so petty, crime which often culminated in crowds flocking to the gruesome spectacle of public hangings at Tyburn Hill (now Marble Arch).

Nor were many of the politicians of the day over-scrupulous and William Makepeace Thackeray, who was fascinated by eighteenth-century life, wrote that 'they swarmed in lewd and naughty practices' and 'took and enjoyed the prizes of politics and the pleasures of social life'.[2] John Wilkes, for example, who was Lord Mayor of

London in 1774 and a Member of Parliament, on and off, between 1757 and 1797, behaved outrageously in his private life. He was a prominent member of the Hell-fire Club, which indulged in extravagant orgies at Medmenham Abbey, the home of Sir Francis Dashwood, and he was involved in the distribution of Thomas Potter's *Essay on Women* which was widely regarded as obscene. Yet he came to be a symbol of free speech and dubbed himself 'a friend of liberty'.[3]

George III was on the throne when Thompson arrived in England and the political scene was largely dominated by the impact of the American War. The king had reigned since 1760 and he was a popular, patriotic and pious monarch, who led an exemplary private life. Strong-willed and stubborn, he had had to deal with six different prime ministers in his first ten years before he found, in 1770, Lord North, who was someone to his liking. He strongly supported Lord North's view that the rebellion across the Atlantic must be quashed, but there were many in England who thought otherwise, supporting the rebels, and arguing for an amicable settlement of the differences. Chief among them were John Wilkes, Edmund Burke and the Marquis of Rockingham, who had been Prime Minister for eleven months between 1765 and 1766. They were backed by a large number of refugees from New England, still loyal to the king, who had settled, temporarily they thought, mainly in London and Bristol.

After 1755 the conduct of the war was in the hands of Lord George Germain, the Secretary of State for the

Colonies in Lord North's cabinet. The third son of the Duke of Dorset, he was born Lord Sackville but he changed his name to Germain in 1770 when he was left a large estate and £20,000 by a friend, Lady Betty Germain, on condition that he change his name. He was a well-built man, 1.8 metres tall, with a blustering and bombastic style of oratory which he often used to try to hide his ignorance. He had, for example, failed to realize, in the winter of 1775, that the St Lawrence River was frozen, so that the four shiploads of stores he had planned to send to General Carleton in Quebec could not be delivered. But he was not only badly briefed; he was also very unpopular. This arose because after the battle of Minden, fought on 1 August 1759, he had apparently disobeyed orders from his commander-in-chief to advance on the retreating French. At the subsequent court martial, he had been found guilty and pronounced unfit to serve His Majesty in any military capacity whatsoever.

The resulting disgrace forced him to lie low on his family estate for some fifteen years but he eventually wheedled his way back into the corridors of power by letting it be known that he was strongly in favour of crushing the rebellion in America. His years of isolation had embittered him and he had become a 'vindictive manipulator of men' – so much so, that, once in power, he organized a large private army to keep him there.

Towards the end of April 1776 Thompson called on Lord George and presented himself as an important loyalist with up-to-date information on the American scene. His case was strengthened by a recommendation from John Wentworth, the Governor of New Hampshire, and by a letter from General Howe which read: 'Benjamin Thompson Esq. having been forced to abandon a competent state in the Province of New Hampshire, from whence he was cruelly drove by persecution and severe Maltreatment, on account of his Loyalty and faithful Efforts to support the Law and promote the service of Government, took refuge in Boston, Where as well as in the Country he has endeavour'd to be useful to His Majesty's service, and is therefore to be considered as deserving of Protection and Favours.'[4]

The meeting was extremely beneficial to both men. Thompson provided Germain with accurate information about the progress of the war which had hitherto been sadly lacking, and Germain gave Thompson an entry into the heart of English society where he could exert considerable influence. He was, once again, in the right place at the right time. The two men also hit it off personally even though one was a worn-out aristocrat and the other an upstart son of a country farmer. Germain included Thompson in his entourage and had him to stay at his country home, Stoneland Lodge, near Tunbridge Wells in Kent, on many occasions. Thompson became a close friend of the family, to the extent that there were rumours about his association with Germain's wife and daughters. It was even suggested that there was a homosexual relationship between the two men. That was probably overdoing it but it is a measure of the extent to which both men were disliked.

They were, nevertheless, extremely useful to each other. When Germain wrote to George III on 15 December 1776, that 'the Loyalty, Integrity, and Ability of Our Trusty and Welbeloved Benjamin Thompson recommends him as Secretary for The Province of Georgia',[5] he was duly appointed to that post. It was a meaningless sinecure with a salary of £100 per annum but it was a measure of Germain's trust in his associate. Quite what Thompson did in his new position is not very clear because, although he was normally a great letter writer there is very little recorded correspondence between 1776 and 1780. He was, however, closely involved in trying to alleviate the plight of some of the other loyalist refugees. Many of them had arrived in England for what they expected to be only a temporary stay, and expecting to be awarded some reparation from the government for the losses they had suffered through their loyalty. Instead they found that they were blamed for not doing more to prevent the rebellion in the first place.

Thompson was responsible for assessing the claims of the refugees and he worked hard to help them but with little tangible result. One of the claimants, Samuel Curwen, had been a Deputy Judge of Admiralty and Crown Provincial Impost Officer in Salem when Thompson was a shop assistant there. He was granted a gratuity of £100 and an annual pension of the same amount. He described Thompson in his diaries as 'a courtier of whom I have never entertained favourable impressions'.[6] Dr John Jeffries, who also kept a diary and who in 1785 was the first man, together with François Blanchard, to cross the English Channel by balloon, also turned to Thompson for help, only to find that he was much more interested in his wife than in his claim.

The job of Secretary to the Province of Georgia was clearly not very onerous because Thompson had enough time to resurrect an earlier interest in gunpowder which had always held some fascination for him. He had used the black powder – unsuccessfully – to make fireworks in his youth, and he wrote that 'no human invention of which we have any authentic records, except, perhaps, the art of printing, has produced such important changes in civil society as the invention of gunpowder'.[7] And so it was that he embarked on an important series of experiments at Stoneland Lodge, probably encouraged by his discussions with Germain on military matters. He was helped by the Revd Ball, the scientifically minded rector of Withyham.

First, he tried to lay to rest the commonly held view that slightly moist gunpowder was more effective in guns than dry powder. The idea was that the heat produced when the moist powder exploded would convert the water into steam and the resulting large increase in volume would increase further the pressure within the gun barrel. Thompson put this to the test by taking small air-bladders from fish, filling them with differing amounts of water and adding them to the gunpowder in cartridges which he then used to fire bullets from a pistol into an oak plank about 2 metres away. When he measured the penetration of the bullets into the oak and the recoil of the pistol, he found that they both decreased as the amount of water in the cartridge increased. He also found a similar decrease when he used other liquids, such as alcohol, turpentine and mercury, instead of water.

Rumford's diagram of his éprouvette which he set up in Lord George Germain's coach house.

Thompson then turned his attention to improving his method of measuring the strength of a charge by firing his bullets into a heavy free-swinging pendulum instead of an oak plank. This was an adaptation of a method first used by Benjamin Robins, a teacher of mathematics and the author of *New Principles of Gunnery* in 1742 and developed further by Charles Hutton, professor of mathematics at the Royal Military Academy at Woolwich in 1778. In Thompson's method he used both a free-swinging gun and a free-swinging pendulum, and he measured the movement of both by attaching tapes to them. His apparatus came to be called an éprouvette (gunpowder-trier), and Thompson used it, for instance, to find the best position for the vent hole in a gun, and to compare the velocity of a bullet when it emerged from the muzzle of the gun and when it impinged on its target. He published his findings in a 99-page paper entitled 'New Experiments upon Gunpowder', in the 1781 volume of the *Philosophical Transactions of the Royal Society*.

The paper was criticized because it contained little or no mention of the earlier work of Robins and Hutton, but its scientific worth was recognized when Thompson was made a Fellow of the Royal Society. The election certificate described him as 'a gentleman well versed in natural knowledge and many branches of polite learning'.[8] This was another large feather in his cap: he was only twenty-seven but he could write FRS after his name. It also brought him into contact with a new group of influential people such as the President of the Society, Sir Joseph Banks. Similar equipment to that used by Robins, Hutton and Thompson is still used for testing the power of explosives; it is known today as a ballistic pendulum.

Thompson was able to widen his experience of gunnery still further in the summer of 1779 when Lord George Germain arranged for him to go on a three-month cruise with the Channel Fleet, in the *Victory* under the command of Sir Charles Hardy. The advertised purpose of this was to allow Thompson to study gunfire from naval cannon and he wrote that he had 'opportunities of making several interesting observations which gave me much new light relative to the action of fired gunpowder'.[9] There were, however, no detailed accounts of what he had done or discovered – adding credence to the view that his main mission had nothing much to do with guns.

Ever since the French and the Spanish had declared war against Britain (in 1778 and 1779 respectively), Germain

HMS *Victory*. (Drawn by Neil Shearer)

had been fighting his own battle with the Earl of Sandwich, the First Lord of the Admiralty, to gain control of the navy, which was not in good shape. It was therefore in Germain's interest to gather any information which he could use to embarrass Sandwich – not difficult, perhaps, since he was a fellow-member with Wilkes of the Hell-fire Club. This is probably what Thompson was doing in the summer of 1779. He was, in fact, back at his old game of spying.

Thompson pulled no punches in the critical and detailed reports which he sent back to Germain. He did not doubt the bravery of the individual commanders but he regarded them as stupid and incompetent. 'I call God and Heaven to witness that it gives me pain when I tell you that I think Sir Charles Hardy is not a fit person to command this great fleet'[10] was not untypical. He was also critical of many of the detailed operational procedures. For example, an error in the use of signalling flags intended to order the fleet into line actually announced that it was payday. Such incompetence eventually led Thompson to design his own signalling system, but the details were never published and nothing came of it. Similarly, his plans for building a new type of frigate carrying 250 men and 40 guns never materialized. If his lurid accounts of what went on in the navy at that time are to be believed, it was lucky that the British fleet had only one brief encounter with the French and Spanish enemy, during which Hardy made for the safety of British harbours as quickly as he could. It was even reported that, when this was happening, the crew on Admiral John Ross's ship wrapped their clothes round the bust of George II so that he 'should not see an English fleet chased up their own Channel'.[11]

Whatever happened, nothing ever seemed to stop Thompson's advancement and late in 1799 he was appointed as deputy to the Inspector General of Provincial Forces, Colonel Alexander Innes, who was stationed in Charleston, South Carolina. This gave Thompson sole administrative responsibility for providing clothing and other stores to all the British armed forces serving in the colonies. As far as clothing was concerned, he bought the uniforms (or the cloth from which they could be made), in London and sold them to the Army in the colonies at the best price he could arrange. This highly speculative operation enabled Thompson, for the first time in his life, to make good money. He was able to take advantage of the fact that silk, widely used in the uniforms, is hygroscopic; thus 50 kilograms of dry silk bought in London would absorb about 10 per cent of its weight in water during the journey across the Atlantic. So there was a considerable profit to be made simply by buying and selling silk by weight. On the other side of the coin, Thompson did use his scientific skills to try to find ways of treating the silk so that it would be more resistant to rotting. The accounting procedures were not very strict and it was taken for granted that the people involved would benefit. Indeed, Thompson tried to increase his share of the cake, at the expense of Colonel Innes's, by suggesting a new method of keeping the books, but Innes accused him of corruption.

It was reported by one of his many detractors that Thompson was making £7,000 per year but no one seems to have objected and in September 1780 he was promoted to the position of Under Secretary of State for the Colonies. This involved him in many important decisions and a great deal of detailed administrative action. The evidence, such as it is, suggests that he promised much but achieved little, and that in some instances he behaved very vindictively towards individuals he disliked.

Henry Laurens, a former president of the Continental Congress, was one such. The Congress sent him to Holland in August 1780 to negotiate a large loan with the Dutch Government, and to encourage them to continue their supply of naval stores and the use of harbours in the Dutch West Indies. Unluckily for him, the boat in which he was travelling was intercepted off Newfoundland by a British warship and Laurens found himself in the Tower of London charged with high treason. Thompson delayed the hearing of his case, and Laurens was so badly treated in the Tower that when he was eventually tried he had to be carried to the court in a sedan chair. He was in the end exchanged as a prisoner of war for Lord Cornwallis. The incident was one of the reasons for the British decision to declare war on Holland in 1780.

But Thompson's days were numbered. The war in America was going badly for the British, and its continuation was leading to high taxes. The government was so unpopular that George III dissolved Parliament and called a general election on 1 September 1780. The government was re-elected but with a majority of just six; the writing was on the wall and the politicians and their

Rumford at the age of thirty.

stooges turned their thoughts to the future. Lord Germain was the most unpopular member of the government so Thompson's position was becoming particularly insecure. He had by this time amassed quite a fortune and this enabled him to buy a commission in the army. So, in February 1781, for a payment of £4,500, he was appointed a lieutenant-colonel in command of the King's American Dragoons. He recruited 366 men, mainly in the early stages at his own expense, though the government did pay a bounty of 3 guineas to every new recruit. There were, too, some severe conditions. The officers had to be gentlemen of education and influence in America who had suffered in their property on account of their loyalty, and Thompson was not allowed to lure men from the navy or any other army unit. He could, however, 'hire out' the regiment to the King or his ministers, and when the regiment was no longer needed for service the remaining officers could go on to half-pay for the rest of their lives.

Thompson employed Captain Daniel Murray to travel to New York to begin recruiting, while he remained as Under Secretary in London. But in the summer of 1781 he gave up his post quite unexpectedly, after occupying it for less than a year. He sailed from England aboard the *Rotterdam* on 7 October to join Murray in New York, but the ship was blown off course, landing at Charleston in South Carolina on 29 December. His sudden departure was somewhat mysterious and untypical of him in that it was not well organized. His affairs, for example, were left in some disorder and had to be tidied up by a friend from his days in Salem, John Fisher, whom Thompson had chosen to succeed him as Under Secretary. Fisher had to sell some of Thompson's possessions to settle unpaid tradesmen's bills, and to stop the allowance that Thompson was paying to the wife of his regimental armourer, no doubt for services rendered.

One possible explanation for Thompson's rapid departure is that he was involved in a French spy scandal in which a Frenchman, Francis Henry de La Motte, had been caught red-handed in possession of detailed British naval plans. Found guilty at his trial, he was drawn and quartered with some pomp at a public ceremony. The source of his information, never actually established, was referred to in his trial as a 'friend in a certain office'[12] and there were many who thought it was Benjamin Thompson.

So Thompson's life, never very placid, had become very complicated, and it did not improve very much when he landed in America, where the war was going very badly for the British. A force of 8,000 men commanded by Lord Cornwallis had been besieged at Yorktown by 16,000 men of General Washington's army and had been prevented from escaping by sea because the British navy was unable to break the French naval blockade. Cornwallis was forced to surrender on 19 October and when Lord North heard the news from Lord Germain on 25 November, he opened his arms, exclaiming wildly, as he paced up and down the apartment during a few minutes – 'Oh God – it's all over.'[13] And so, to all intents and purposes, it was. Germain resigned in February 1782 and was, rather reluctantly, granted a peerage by George III, becoming Viscount Sackville of Drayton. The poor man was haunted by animosity in the Lords as he had been in the Commons, and Lord North was replaced as Prime Minister by Lord Rockingham on 20 March.

Delayed in Charleston, Thompson did not arrive in New York until 11 April, when he turned his attention to completing the recruitment for his regiment. This was made difficult by the parlous state of affairs from the British point of view, but he offered 10 guineas to newly enlisted men, and was helped by being allowed to take under his wing the remnants of other forces, such as the Queen's Rangers. By 1 August the King's American Dragoons regiment was ready for service and they were greatly honoured when they were reviewed by the King's third son, the sixteen-year-old Prince William Henry (the future King William IV), who presented their colours to them. Their commanding officer, aged thirty, wrote that his troops were 'one of the crack corps in the army'[14] and 'that he would not be ashamed to show them in Hyde Park'.[15]

Their first action was on 27 September at Lloyd's Neck, 8 kilometres from Huntingdon and 65 from New York, where they demolished the existing redoubt, evacuated the post and removed the stores before establishing their headquarters at Huntingdon. Thompson continued to write to Sackville and constantly emphasized the quality of his regiment – but local people told a different tale. They reported how Thompson built barracks for his men on a burial ground belonging to a local chapel, and deliberately pitched his tent over the grave of the Revd Ebenezer Percy, a well-known supporter of American liberty, in order that he 'might tred on the damned old rebel's head whenever he went in and out'.[16] The gravestones were used by Thompson's men to build baking ovens, which resulted in local people receiving loaves of bread with the names of their dead relatives inscribed in the crusts. No wonder they regarded Thompson as the devil incarnate and called his camp Fort Golgotha. To make matters worse, he was living in some style with two English servants, six horses and a negro groom, and spent most of his time hunting deer and travelling around the countryside in his own grand phaeton. This was a measure of how much the fighting had declined and that the war was in its last stages.

A peace treaty had been signed by Great Britain and the United States on 30 November 1782 but it was not fully ratified until 3 September 1783, when Britain settled her differences with France, Spain and Holland and the Treaty of Paris was signed, finally bringing to an end eight years of war. All the parties were ready for peace. The rebels, keeping faith with the ideals summarized in the Declaration of Independence signed by the thirteen colonies on 4 July

1776, had won the day. The United States were recognized, with the Mississippi River and the Great Lakes as their western boundary, and the sometimes rather painful business of building up a democratic system of government began. But it was not easy to ensure the self-evident truths 'that all men are created equal; that they are endowed by their Creator with certain inalienable rights; that amongst these are life, liberty and the pursuit of happiness' as the Declaration demanded. Those who had remained loyal to George III were not well treated and it was estimated that 80,000 people had emigrated or been banished. In some states, too, it took ten years before all the anti-loyalist legislation was repealed. Nor was the future in Europe very certain. The British National Debt had grown by £100,000,000 and the French Revolution was just around the corner.

THREE

BAVARIAN ADVENTURE

The end of the war meant that Thompson, in common with many others, had to think again about his future. He was only thirty years old but he had already built up something of a reputation as a statesman, scientist, soldier and spy, but what was he to do next? He decided that soldiering was probably his best bet. He had taken every opportunity, and indeed used false or outrageously exaggerated claims, to let everyone know how good he was at it, and he tried to get his King's American Dragoons involved in action in the West Indies, Nova Scotia and India. When those plans did not materialize, he looked around the world for other possible trouble-spots, writing to Major Murray that 'if there should be a War, I shall engage in it, on one side or the other, I don't care a farthing which'.[1] His chosen venue was Vienna in central Europe, where the on-going conflict between Austria, Prussia and Russia on the one hand and France on the other was always likely to erupt.

Before setting off, Thompson prepared the ground as thoroughly as he could. He used his old contacts in England to get himself promoted to full colonel, even though he had only served in the army for about sixteen months (he then retired on half-pay for the rest of his life); he had his portrait painted by Thomas Gainsborough in full military regalia; he obtained letters of introduction to Sir Robert Murray Keith, the British Ambassador in Vienna, from Lord North and William Fraser, his successor as Under Secretary of State; he bought three fine American horses; and he engaged a groom and a servant. Thus equipped, though speaking no German and only a little French, he set off from Dover on 17 September 1783. On the same boat were Henry Laurens and the distinguished historian Edward Gibbon, who recognized his versatility by referring to him somewhat sarcastically in a letter as Mr Secretary, Colonel, Admiral, Philosopher Thompson. Their rough passage – almost everyone was sea-sick and the boat had to land at Boulogne instead of Calais – may well have been a portent for the future but Thompson's luck was not going to forsake him now. It hardly ever did.

He travelled on to Strasbourg where by chance Prince Maximilian of Zweibrücken, later to rule Bavaria, was reviewing his troops. Among the spectators was Thompson, mounted on one of his horses and wearing the full uniform of an English colonel. The Prince, noticing this distinguished figure, asked for a meeting to be arranged. It then transpired that the Prince's regiment had fought at Yorktown and that many of the officers on parade had seen service in the American War of Independence. This shared interest, though they had served on different sides, led to a lifelong friendship between Thompson and the Prince.

Thompson arrived in Vienna in 1784 but he was thwarted in his aim to advance his military career when he found everything unexpectedly peaceful, so he played for time by travelling to Venice and Trieste. It was by a stroke of luck – a 'beneficent Deity'[2] in his own words – that he met by chance the seventy-year-old wife of General Bourghausen, a friend of Joseph II, Emperor of Germany. 'This excellent person', he told a friend, 'conceived a regard for me; she gave me the wisest advice, made my ideas take a new direction, and opened my eyes to other kinds of glory than that of victory in battle.'[3] And so it was that, armed with a letter of introduction from Prince Maximilian to his uncle Carl Theodore, the then Elector of Bavaria, Thompson moved on to Munich, the Bavarian capital, where, surprisingly, he was appointed as a colonel to be both aide-de-camp to the Elector and tutor to his illegitimate son, the Count von Bretzenheim.

He could not take up the post immediately because he was still technically employed by King George III so he had to return to England to seek permission to accept the new offer. That he still enjoyed considerable influence and undiminished powers of persuasion is shown by the fact that he was not only granted permission, he was also knighted. This was probably as much of a surprise to him as to anyone else but the honour was conferred because the British government wanted to improve relations with Bavaria to try to lessen the influence of France.

It was also suggested that part of the deal required Thompson to act as a spy, secretly passing any information he could glean while in Europe to Sir Robert Keith in Vienna. Arrangements were therefore made for the two men to become acquainted with each other's handwriting, and it was agreed that any letters containing secret information would be addressed to their bankers and left unsigned. Sir Keith, however, soon became very suspicious that Thompson was not keeping his side of the agreement, and arranged for him to be 'watched' by Thomas Walpole, the official British ambassador in Munich, with whom Thompson soon fell out.

All this linking of honours with spying was very reminiscent of Thompson's meeting with Governor Wentworth in New Hampshire eleven years earlier. Did it all happen because Thompson had such a magnetic personality or was it simply fortune favouring the brave? One of the factors involved was certainly Thompson's egotistical self-presentation, which often strayed far from the truth. In the diploma recording his Grant of Arms as a knight, for example, he claims to have been a colonel in a regiment of militia in New Hampshire, and that his ancestors were the owners of Thompson Island at the entrance to Boston harbour. Both claims are false, but that everything might be possible for Thompson was borne out by the comment on his knighthood in a letter from Edward Winslow, a friend of Major Murray. He wrote: 'Well done Sir Benjamin! The next news we hear will probably be that he has mounted a Baloon – taken his flight from Bavaria – and is Chief Engineer to an Aerial Queen.'[4]

Bavaria (or Bayern in German) is today an administrative region in Germany with a population of 11,000,000 and

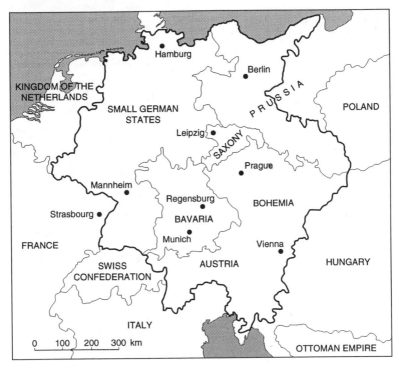

The boundaries of the Holy Roman Empire in 1780.

with Munich as its capital. In the 1760s it was one of many independent states of the Holy Roman Empire, which had been founded through conquest by Charlemagne in 800, and which at its height extended over most of Central and Western Europe. In the area now regarded as Germany, the two largest states were Austria and Prussia, with Saxony, the Palatinate (stretching from Belgium in the west to Austria in the east), and Bavaria next in size. There were also some smaller city-states such as Brunswick, Mainz and Cologne.

Maximilian III had been Elector of Bavaria but on his death in 1778 that state had combined with the Palatinate, with its Elector Carl Theodore as joint ruler. He had worked hard to improve standards in the Palatinate, but he was less interested in Bavaria and was very reluctant to move to Munich. Elderly and apathetic, he was very set in his ways; easily influenced by his mistresses and his favourite relatives; and dominated by the Catholic Church, in the form of Father Ignaz Frank, his Jesuit confessor. So even though he could be quite charming, he was neither a popular nor an effective Elector and he did not have a male heir.

He provided Thompson with a well-staffed, palatial villa in the *Schwabinger Gasse*, which he was to share with the Russian ambassador, but advised him to lie low for a while and to improve his German and French. So Sir Benjamin spent the next four years settling in to his new surroundings. He wrote that he admired 'the frank cordiality which so eminently distinguishes the Bavarian nation'[5] and the free and easy relations between the sexes were to his liking. It was almost inevitable that he would quickly build up his reputation as a womanizer by having affairs with two sisters, Countess Baumgarten and Countess Nogarola. The former, a beautiful but fat ex-mistress of Carl Theodore, in due course bore Thompson a daughter, Sophia. The latter, the younger sister, was slim and intelligent but not good-looking; she became a lifelong loving companion who engaged him in philosophical discussions and helped him with his writing.

But however attractive and forward some of the ladies might be, it did not take Thompson long to conclude that the state itself was very backward. The government was corrupt, extravagant and incompetent, taxes were high, trade and industry were stagnant, there were more monasteries than factories, the army was in disarray, there was far too much crime and far too many beggars – and no one seemed to care very much. The French traveller Kaspar Risbeck wrote that 'the court in Munich is enveloped in such a thick, motley and glittering swarm of Ministers, Councillors, Intendants and Commandants that one can hardly see through it' and 'most of the rich families know of no other use for their money but to eat, to drink, to whore, and to gamble'.[6]

It was clear, then, that the state was ripe for reform on all sides. Luckily for the majority of the people, the Elector was quite glad to let Thompson try to do the reforming while he sat back and took the hoped-for credit. Realizing that he could not do everything at once and that it would be difficult to tackle the Church, Thompson turned his attention to the reorganization of the army and on 7 February 1788 he submitted a detailed plan to the Elector. This was accepted with open arms, and, to help him in the task, Thompson was appointed Minister of War, with the rank of major-general, to replace Count Belderbusch, who was sent to Mannheim as military governor. For good measure, Thompson also became Minister of Police,

Chamberlain to the Court and a state councillor. Moreover, it was agreed that if he could achieve his reforms and save money he could keep that money for himself.

The army was indeed in poor order. It was made up of about 18,000 men in thirty regiments but was extremely top heavy, with about a quarter of the soldiers being officers. There were several general field marshals, and even a great admiral commanding a few ships on the Rhine. The other ranks were recruited by conscripting unwilling, ill-educated peasants from country villages, sometimes by adopting devious methods such as blackmail and kidnapping. It was also commonplace for courts to impose sentences involving a period in prison together with a period in the army.

The soldiers were paid enough to cover the cost of their food, but they had to buy much of their clothing and equipment themselves and were constantly in debt. To repay their debts they had to borrow from their officers or hire themselves out, with the officers acting as intermediaries, for civilian work. They were subject to harsh discipline maintained by the use of the whip, chain-lash and even the gallows. No wonder they were something of a rabble, who subjected local civilians to a reign of terror involving begging, theft, rape and even murder.

Thompson summarized his intention as 'to endeavour to unite the interest of the soldier with the interest of civil society, and to render the military force, even in time of peace, subservient to the public good'.[7] To that end he persuaded Carl Theodore to forbid the sentencing of criminals to army service; he increased the soldiers' pay and provided them with free clothing and equipment; he allowed them to earn money outside the army and to keep it for themselves; he gave them leave if they had to go home to help with sowing or harvesting; he humanized the disciplinary regimes; he set up schools to educate the soldiers and their families; he established a military academy for the training of officers and a veterinary school to improve the supply of horses; he reorganized the manufacture of cannon in the arsenals at Mannheim and Munich; and he ordered that every regiment should have its own military band which would play not only on special occasions but whilst the soldiers were at their normal daily work.

He also made great strides in running the army more efficiently so that costs could be kept under control. He recognized that it might be possible to reduce two of the major expenses – food and clothing – and he applied his scientific mind to the problems. This involved him in original research in nutrition and in the thermal conductivity of the materials used in making clothing.

As far as food was concerned he wanted to discover how to feed a large number of people effectively and efficiently. One of the first practical steps he introduced was to direct each garrison to organize its own vegetable gardens, and individual non-commissioned officers and privates were given plots of land, 33 square metres in area, to keep as allotments. Thompson also provided detailed information about what vegetables to grow, how best to grow them and how to prepare them for the table. He was an early advocate of crop rotation, strongly recommending 'new' crops such as turnips and clover, and in 1796 he wrote an essay, 'Of Food: and Particularly of Feeding the Poor', which refers to the 'science of nutrition' and gives much sound practical advice of which any modern cook might be proud.

When it came to clothing the soldiers, Thompson realized that he had to decide which material was best for making uniforms. He therefore began a series of experiments designed to measure the thermal conductivity of different materials. To do this he invented what he called a passage thermometer, which consisted of a normal thermometer surrounded by a glass jacket closed at both ends. To test each material, he packed it in the tube around the central thermometer and placed the whole in boiling water until the temperature recorded on the thermometer was 70°C. He then placed the whole in a bath of ice and measured how long it took for the temperature to drop to 10°C. He compared different materials, such as silk, feathers, wool, cotton and fur, using equal weights, and also studied individual materials by packing them in different ways and using them with different amounts of added water. His measurements led him to conclude that it was the amount of air trapped within a material which had the greatest effect on its conductivity. A fluffy material like a woollen blanket or an eiderdown would keep you warmer on a cold day than a tightly woven one such as cotton, linen or silk. Thompson had discovered that heat was transmitted by the movement of the molecules within a gas in what are now known as convection currents, though that term was not used until 1834 when it was introduced by the British chemist William Prout. Thompson reported his findings to the Royal Society in 1792 and he was awarded one of its highest honours, the Copley medal.

The practical outcome of all this work was the decision to simplify the design of the army uniforms and to make them of cotton for the summer and of wool for the winter. This has been commonplace for a long time, but it was very new in 1792. Indeed, Thompson found it very difficult to implement the change because the existing manufacturers were not in favour of it. Such hostility to change was just as common in 1792 as it has been ever since, but Thompson was a man of determination and he bypassed the manufacturers by setting up what he called a military workhouse in Mannheim to make the uniforms independently. This policy was not at first very successful because of the difficulty of finding suitable workers but that problem was eventually solved and workhouses became a dominant part of Thompson's reforms and of Bavarian life.

The uniform manufacturers were not the only group to resist the reforms. Many officers resigned when they found that discipline was being relaxed and their opportunities to make money were being curtailed. Others objected to the expense of Thompson's schemes and accused him of maladministration. So he decided to put his record to the test and on 1 June 1792 he produced a report for the Elector, summarizing what his four years of work had achieved. A Commission of Inquiry, set up to look into the matter, did not support Thompson wholeheartedly but he was not deterred, and he had already turned his attention to the second stage of his reform programme, to tackle the longstanding problems caused by beggars.

It was estimated that perhaps 5 per cent of Bavarians relied on begging to avoid complete destitution. In the big cities it was almost impossible to avoid beggars, many of whom operated in gangs which ruled their own allotted area. Some of them were strong but idle, men and women who were part of Mafia-like organizations which handed down their know-how from generation to generation. Others might have had some excuse because they were old or disabled, and some were, it seemed, children who had been stolen from their parents and deliberately maimed or blinded so that they could beg more effectively. This social canker had been allowed to fester over many years and had come to be accepted as an unavoidable evil, but Thompson was brave enough to declare war on the beggars – he called them 'detestable vermin'[8] – and his reform programme once again gained the Elector's support.

His bold but simple plan was to round up all the beggars and to employ them in workhouses making military uniforms. The plan was put into effect like a military operation early in the morning on New Year's Day 1790 when the officers and non-commissioned officers from three regiments of the army, accompanied by local magistrates, combed the streets of Munich with orders to arrest every beggar they could find. Within an hour they had cleared the streets, Thompson himself arresting the first with his own hands.

The beggars were first taken to the Town Hall where detailed lists of names and other particulars were made before they were sent back home with instructions to report the following day to the military workhouse, or house of industry as Thompson preferred to call it. They were promised that, in return for their labour, they would be provided with a good warm dinner, necessary training, wages and medical care.

The main workhouse was based on an earlier institution organized by Rumford in Mannheim, but which had been only partially successful. Situated in a suburb called Au, on the outskirts of Munich, it was in a building that had been first a monastery and then a factory; Thompson had it renovated and enlarged by the addition of a kitchen, refectory, bakehouse and a number of workshops. The

The original military workhouse in Munich.

square building enclosed a paved courtyard, itself entered by a passage over which a sign reading 'No Alms Will be Received Here' was placed. It was equipped with all the necessary items for preparing hemp, flax, cotton and wool, for spinning them into threads, for weaving and for sewing and knitting. The day-to-day running of the workhouse was in the hands of a central committee of local worthies and professionals aided by sixteen district committees. They ensured that the regime was benign and based it on the principle of making the inmates happy before trying to make them virtuous, as opposed to the generally accepted method of dealing with miscreants by trying to make them virtuous in the hope that this would automatically bring happiness in its train.

Men, women and children over five years old were all given suitable tasks according to their ability, and they were expected to work between twelve and fourteen hours each day. They were trained in a wide variety of skills, as required, and paid, many of them on a piecework basis. There was a school in the dining room, which ran for an hour in the morning and an hour in the afternoon; it was mainly for children but anyone could attend. When Thompson found that he needed to increase production he organized out-workers who worked in their own homes, and set up a ticket system that allowed them to collect a hot meal from the workhouse. If a healthy beggar did not come to work, he was not paid or fed; if ill, the situation was looked into by a district committee. Any beggar who returned to the old ways on the street was re-arrested.

Thompson's unique social experiment was a great success. It had been costly to establish and had required money from his own pocket as well as from the government and from voluntary contributions, but after five or six years the scheme began to make a profit. What's more, many of the original beggars had completely changed their ways and had been reabsorbed into the community as self-reliant and useful citizens. Thompson's aim of producing 'a total and radical change in the morals, manners and customs of this debauched and abandoned race'[9] had largely been achieved. He had also become something of an idol to them – so much so that, when he fell ill, they set aside an hour to pray for him after they had finished their day's work. Unhappily, at the same time, his success and public exposure was arousing more and more hostility, much of it springing from jealousy and envy, from those who thought that the activities of this foreign upstart ought to be curtailed.

There were, however, no signs of that happening because even before he had finished his reforms of the army and the beggars, he had dreamt up another grand enterprise. This was to have a lasting impact on life in Munich and is still there today in the form of the English Garden. His idea was to turn a derelict area of marshy ground on the banks of the River Isar north of the town into something like Kew Gardens in London, which had been started in 1759 as a private garden by Princess Augusta, the mother of George III. The area, known as the Hirschanger or the Red Deer Grassy Plains, had been used traditionally as a hunting-ground for the Electors and was much appreciated for that purpose by Carl Theodore, but Thompson persuaded him to agree to its conversion into a garden which was originally intended to be called Theodore Park. Work began in August 1789 under the control of Friedrich Ludwig von Sckell, who had studied landscape gardening in Paris and London. The labour was provided by the Bavarian army and no expense was spared to create all the paths, bridges, dams, lakes, lawns, trees, shrubs and flowers, together with Greek temples, a Chinese pagoda, a concert hall, summerhouses, cafés, a racecourse and an amphitheatre. After a formal dedication by the Elector in May 1790, it was opened to the public a year later, and Thompson had provided the citizens of Munich, rich and poor alike, with the finest park in Europe. They commemorated the event in 1795 by erecting a magnificent, quadrangular monument made of Bavarian freestone and marble. On one side there are two figures representing the Genius of Plenty leading Bavaria and strewing her path with flowers. The German inscription beneath has been translated as

> Pause, saunterer! Enjoyment is heightened by gratitude. A suggestive wink from Charles Theodore, Seized on with genius, taste and love by Rumford, the friend of Mankind, Has transformed this once waste spot Into what thou now seest about thee.[10]

The opposite side carries a bust of Rumford in alabaster above the inscription:

The monument to Count Rumford in the English Garden, Munich.

To him Who rooted out the most disgraceful public evils, Idleness and Mendicity. Who to the Poor gave Succour, Work and Good Habits, and to the Youth of the Fatherland so many chances of Instruction. Go, saunterer, and strive to match him in Spirit and Deed, and us in Gratitude.[11]

Yet the garden, just after its completion, had caused a serious rift between Thompson and the Munich City Council. The councillors had not been officially involved in planning or building the garden but it had been given to them, legally, by the Elector when it was opened, and they thought they were in charge. They were then very upset when they found that Thompson had distributed – without the Council's permission – a copy of a letter praising the garden, which had been sent to the Elector by a group of citizens. It all seemed relatively harmless but the subsequent reactions of all the parties concerned blew it up out of all proportion.

The Council's demand that the letter be withdrawn and their threat to prosecute all the signatories so enraged Thompson that he immediately complained to the Elector, who dismissed the mayor and several of the leading councillors, stopped their pay and banned them from holding any further office for life. Thompson was not placated, and the Elector agreed to his further request that those involved should be humiliated by being forced to kneel before a portrait of the Elector and ask for pardon.

This unfortunate, and rather silly, episode only served to worsen the love-hate relationship that had developed between Thompson and the Bavarian people. Thompson was still, however, well in with the Elector who showered him with even more favours and offices. He made him a privy councillor in March 1790, awarded him a lifelong pension five months later and promoted him to Chief of the General Staff in February 1792. Then, to crown all that, the Elector, acting as vice-regent after the death of the Austrian Emperor Leopold II until the appointment of his successor Francis II four months later, took the fleeting opportunity to promote Thompson, on 9 May 1792, to the rank and dignity of the Imperial Counts of the Holy Roman Empire, making him a Knight of the White Eagle. Sir Benjamin Thompson FRS chose the title Count Rumford, after the old name of the town in New Hampshire where he had left his wife and daughter sixteen years earlier.

The new count was living in stirring times, and turmoil was beginning to spread throughout Europe. Rousseau's 1762 paradox that 'man is born free; and everywhere he is in chains'[12] still made an impact, and the French Revolution, encouraged by the storming of the Bastille on 14 July 1789, was well under way. In April 1792 France declared war against Austria, and in July Prussia, allied with Austria, declared war on France. In October the French invaded the Rhineland and in November defeated the Austrians at Jemappes; in the Edict of Fraternity they offered to give armed assistance to any peoples wanting to overthrow their rulers. To emphasize the point, Louix XVI was executed on 21 January 1793 and his wife Marie Antoinette met the same fate on 16 October 1793.

These events caused alarm bells to ring in Bavaria, as elsewhere, and support for the ageing Carl Theodore, who had adopted a policy of appeasement, began to decline as support increased for his nephew the Duke of Zwei-brücken, who was next in line. The duke was the older brother of Thompson's friend Prince Maximilian, and he had for some time been in favour of strengthening the military capability of the army instead of using it for building gardens. As his position strengthened, so Carl Theodore's grew weaker.

This had a dramatic effect on the standing of the new Count Rumford. A trusted adviser to Theodore, he had reformed the army – but he had made many enemies in the process. All his exertions had taken their toll; he suffered bouts of ill-health – 'putrid bilious disorders'[13] as he once

called them – and he wrote to friends saying that he was
weary and would like to retreat from public life in Bavaria.
The outcome was that the Elector granted him leave to go
to Italy for a recuperative holiday and he left in March
1793, shortly after France had declared war on Great
Britain and Holland.

He travelled in some style, with much baggage, sending
many servants ahead to make arrangements for his arrival,
but he had no fixed plans and for the first time in his life he
was free to follow his fancies, which were, in the main,
science and invention, social issues involving the well-being
of the poor, and ladies. In Florence he took the opportunity
of the loan of a laboratory to experiment on the nature of
shadows cast by different coloured lights, on the nature
of complementary colours, and on the thermal conductivity of
steam. In Milan he met Sir Charles Blagden, the secretary
of the Royal Society, who was holidaying in Italy. In Pavia he
talked with Count Alessandro Volta, the Professor of physics
at the University, who became famous for his invention of
the first practical electric battery, the Voltaic pile, in 1799.
In Verona he advised on the rebuilding of the kitchens in the
hospitals of La Pietà and La Misericordia, and arranged to
supply the former with clothing from the workhouse in
Munich. In Naples he was ill again, with still more prayers
for his health being offered up in the Munich workhouse.

For the rest, he consorted with his lady friends. Much of
the time was spent with Countess Nogarola, who was living
in Verona with her children while her husband, still in
Bavaria, was preparing the defences of Mannheim. But he

also met Lady Palmerston, Lady Elizabeth Webster and Lady Bolingbroke. When he was away from Lady Palmerston, even for only a few days, he felt 'quite lonesome and melancholy';[14] he discussed politics and morality with Lady Webster, but so far as Lady Bolingbroke was concerned, he wrote that he 'did not know what I might have been tempted to do to cheat away her tedious lingering hours'.[15]

This was all very much to Rumford's liking but he was still in the pay of Carl Theodore and officially on convalescent leave, so after almost sixteen months, in July 1794 he reluctantly returned to Munich. There was something of a hero's welcome with large crowds, mainly consisting of the poor and lowly, turning out to greet him. In response he organized a successful fête in the English garden for 1,800 poor people, which was attended by 80,000 visitors.

That was pleasing but he found, unfortunately, that from his point of view the political scene had deteriorated. Carl Theodore was still the Elector and still friendly, but he was now getting very old; his wife had recently died and he had married a very young Austrian princess. More importantly, his power was being continually undermined by the activities of the Duke of Zweibrücken and his supporters. It was obvious that there would no longer be an official position for Rumford and he felt lonely and isolated. He invited Lady Palmerston to stay in August and it is a measure of the lax morals of the age that, shortly after leaving him, she wrote, very cheekily, to ask whether he had yet slept with the new young Electress.

The answer was that he hadn't, but his letters to Lady Palmerston show that he was simply hanging around in the forlorn hope that his fortune might change for the better. He spent his time making improvements in the workhouse by experimenting with the cooking and feeding methods, planning an extension to the English Garden, writing the first five of his long series of essays on the work he had done, and hosting lavish parties for up to a hundred guests in his home. But for a man with such energy he had too little to do and too little power. So it was a happy release when the Elector gave him leave to go to London for six months.

He left Munich on 13 October 1795, some twelve years after he had first arrived. It was the end of this particular adventure. What had this English-speaking American Protestant achieved in a foreign Catholic country? One commentator wrote that he had 'made noble attempts to apply intelligence and scientific knowledge to improve the lot of soldier and citizen in a land that was not his own'.[16] The contemporary English poet Thomas J. Mathias put it in rather florid verse, and with plenty of poetic licence, in 1794:

> Yet all shall read, and all that page approve,
> When public spirit meets with public love.
> Thus late where poverty with rapine dwelt,
> Rumford's kind genius the Bavarian felt,
> Not by romantic charities beguiled,
> But calm in project and in mercy mild;

Where'er his wisdom guided, none withstood,
Content with peace and practicable good
Round him the labourers throng, the nobles wait,
Friend of the poor and guardian of the state.

A more balanced epithet might be: 'He championed the poor, but antagonized too many of the others.'

THE COUNTESS

Rumford's visit to England did not get off to a very good start because he was driving in London when he was robbed outside St Paul's Cathedral and he lost a large trunk full of his papers. Some of them were recovered when he offered a reward of 10 guineas, but most were never seen again. The motive for the robbery was never firmly established. Some thought it might be related to his supposed spying activities in Bavaria and others that it was simply an attempt to get money. Rumford, however, believed that the theft had a political motive based on the increasing divergence of views between the Bavarian and British governments. Such differences, coupled with the memories which some people had of Rumford when they knew him as Benjamin Thompson and general feelings of resentment now that he was a Count, also meant that he was very much *persona non grata*. Many of his enemies wondered why he had come back to Britain at all and were very suspicious of his motives and his aspirations. All this made Rumford feel very isolated and sorry for himself, so he tried to drown his sorrows in hard work.

Looking on the brighter side, he was happy to renew his acquaintance with Lady Palmerston and he poured out his woes to her. 'Would to God my sufferings were at an end,' he wrote, 'but the idea of leaving my reputation a prey to those infernal wretches who never cease to persecute me drives me to distraction.'[1] He also looked forward to meeting his daughter Sarah, whom he had left in America, and who was now twenty-one years old. There had been a fruitless contact between them in 1792 when a Mr Stacey arrived in Munich carrying a letter of introduction to Count Rumford from his old friend Loammi Baldwin. The purpose of Mr Stacey's unexpected visit was to ask the count for permission to marry his daughter. She was, at the time, under twenty-one years old, so this was simply a traditional advance, but Rumford would not even countenance the idea and sent poor Mr Stacey packing.

The ice had, however, been broken and it seemed that the death of Rumford's wife in January 1792 opened the way for him to consider reconciliation with his daughter. So he wrote to Loammi Baldwin on 18 January 1793 saying that he would like to re-establish relations with Sarah, and he began to send her money on a regular basis. After being deserted by her father, she had been brought up by her mother until she became too ill to cope, and Sarah, aged just four, went to live in an aunt's home, where she was mainly looked after by a slave girl to whom she became very attached. Loammi Baldwin and his wife, and later their son James F. Baldwin, kept a close eye on her, as did the Revd Dr Joseph Willard, President of Harvard College in Cambridge.

Later in life, when she was sixty-eight and living in Paris, Sarah wrote an unpublished autobiography entitled 'Memoirs of a Lady, written by herself'. In it she describes 'the most happy circumstances of a country life',[2] her 'many agreeable acquaintances',[3] 'pony rides and lonely meditation in pleasant woods',[4] and records being 'destitute of proper earthly protection, but of being favoured by a divine Providence'.[5] The book is illustrated by some of her own sketches which show that she had inherited her father's drawing skills. The one important thing that was missing from her young life was a good education. She had spent some time at Mrs Snow's boarding-school in Boston; it was essentially a finishing school with the emphasis on dancing and deportment but she had never really started. Loammi Baldwin wrote to Rumford that 'Sarah has improved greatly on the opportunities she has had'[6] but, educationally, these had been distinctly limited. And she had not been helped when she became ill after her mother's death in 1792, when Sarah was eighteen years old. She was then forced to go to live with the Baldwins.

It was not until the autumn of 1795 that Rumford plucked up enough courage to write, first, to his old mother, sending her some money, and then to Sarah to ask if she would come to live with him in London. She consequently sailed in the *Charlestown* from Boston at the end of January 1796, arriving in March after a six-week voyage. She was twenty-two and she brought with her a letter, almost a recommendation, from Loammi Baldwin saying that 'she possesses a noble mind and wants nothing but the aid of her father to make her accomplished'.[7]

Such a meeting between father and daughter was bound to be traumatic and there were obvious disappointments on both sides. Sarah had in her mind's eye a dashing soldier with a sword; when she found her father thin and pale, she collapsed in tears. Rumford remarked that Sarah was better looking than he had expected, which was not much of a compliment, and his hopes that she would slip easily into the sort of society that he frequented in London were dashed when he found, not surprisingly, that she was a distinctly country girl. He was living in a large hotel in Pall Mall with Aichner, his Bavarian valet, but he arranged for Sarah to stay at Mrs Luckington's boarding-house close by along with her maid Anymeetle, whom he had hired for her from Munich.

Her lack of social graces soon became apparent. At the opera and at dinner parties she made such outrageous comments that her father begged her to keep quiet. On a shopping expedition with her maid she bought, among other things, some very expensive lace and six pairs of fancy shoes, which her father regarded as an extravagant and rather tasteless waste of his money. Her execution of the curtsy was more American than English and not always well timed, and on one occasion she curtsied to the housekeeper whom she had mistaken for the hostess. Such incidents caused Rumford much embarrassment, and he sought to improve matters by sending Sarah to an upper-class boarding-school run by the Marquise de Chabann, a French refugee, in Barnes Terrace. She also had lessons at Ashley's riding school.

Meanwhile Rumford had been immersing himself in his writing and with the help of Lord Sheffield, a friend of

Edward Gibbon and an MP, he found a publisher, T. Cadell Jun. and W. Davies, of the Strand. This enabled his first essay, 'An Account of an Establishment for the Poor at Munich', to go on sale in January 1796. Two more essays followed in quick succession. Essay II was entitled 'Of the Fundamental Principles on which General Establishments for the Relief of the Poor may be Formed in all Countries', and Essay III 'Of Food; and Particularly of Feeding the Poor'. These three essays were summarizing reports of the work he had overseen in Bavaria, but Essay IV, 'Of Chimney Fire-places, with Proposals for Improving them to Save Fuel; to Render Dwelling Houses more Comfortable and Salubrious, and Effectively to Prevent Chimneys from Smoking', covered new ground, probably driven by the sight of so many smoking chimneys in London and the consequent air pollution. There was, indeed, a popular rhyme which ran: 'A smoky house and a scolding wife, Are two of the greatest ills of life'.[8]

In a fulsome dedication of his publication to His Most Serene Highness The Elector Palatine, Reigning Duke of Bavaria, Rumford concluded that he 'was anxious to have the opportunity of testifying, in a public manner, my gratitude to your most Serene Electoral Highness for all your kindness to me; and more especially for the distinguished honour you have done me by selecting and employing me as an instrument in your hands of doing good'.

Rumford was prolific, but he was not a good writer, because he was extremely long-winded and tedious, and his obvious attempts to clarify a point were commonly counter-productive. He wrote as if addressing a rather stupid child and his essays make for heavy reading. On eating a pudding of his own recipe, for example, he managed: 'The pudding is to be eaten with a knife and fork, beginning at the circumference of the slice, and approaching regularly towards the centre, each piece of pudding being taken up with the fork, and dipped into the butter, or dipped into it *in part only*, as is commonly the case, before it is carried into the mouth.'[9]

Nevertheless, the books were full of original and practical ideas well ahead of the times. They were, therefore, very successful and brought him both fame and wealth and encouraged him to go on to produce many more. Fortunately, he was much more practical and effective when implementing his ideas than when writing about them and he travelled all over England, Scotland and Ireland advising institutions such as hospitals on how best to care for their patients. He also offered his services to individuals, redesigning, for example, Lady Palmerston's fireplaces.

Such activities brought him still greater wealth but, even with money in the bank and Sarah in the country, he was clearly not entirely happy in England. Anxious about the future, he went so far as to write to Loammi Baldwin to enquire whether he might be welcome back in America. 'Should I be kindly received?' he wrote. 'Are the remains of Party spirit and political persecutions done away with? Would it be necessary to ask leave of the State?'[10] Loammi's reply encouraged him to return. 'You would realize a hearty welcome from all your old friends and citizens in general. . . . Pray, come and see your kind mother. Make us a visit, if you do no more',[11] he wrote. But nothing came of it.

At about the same time Rumford was beginning to decide that his days as spy, statesman and soldier were over and that his future lay in science. He therefore decided to back two horses at once by offering, in July 1796, to establish prize funds at both the Royal Society in London and the American Academy of Arts and Sciences in Boston. He proposed to give the former £1,000 and the latter $5,000 so that the interest from the capital could be used to award prizes to the inventors of new devices associated with heating or lighting which would 'tend most to promote the good of mankind'.[12] There were a few awkward details, such as the fact that Rumford specified that he should be the first winner of the prizes, but once these had been sorted out, Rumford Medals were struck – and they are still

The Rumford medal awarded by the Royal Society.

awarded by both institutions today.

Any ideas that Rumford had for the future were, however, soon thrown into disarray because by 13 August he was quite unexpectedly back in Munich. During his supposed six-months leave in England there had been some dramatic changes in Bavaria with the escalation of warfare between the French and the Austrians who were fighting on many fronts all over the region. Munich, although anxious to remain neutral, was threatened by the Austrians, 65 kilometres to the north, and by the French, 33 kilometres to the west. The situation was so serious that arrangements were being made to remove art treasures and official documents, and many foreign diplomats had already left the city. Carl Theodore was still the Elector, but he had regained more independence and authority following the deaths of Father Ignaz Frank and the Duke of Zweibrücken, but he was old and frightened. He was in fact planning to leave Munich but he decided to turn once again to Rumford in his hour of need. He therefore sent a messenger to London in late July, beseeching Rumford to return to Bavaria to deal with the impending crisis.

Rumford always saw an opportunity in any situation, however desperate it might appear, so he set about making the necessary arrangements for another journey to Munich. He decided rather reluctantly to take Sarah with him, which meant that he had to hire two coaches and extra servants, and he tried to work out the best route across Europe to avoid the fighting that was already taking place. He also bought a fine English horse to take as a present for Countess Nogarola.

The party left Yarmouth on 24 July and their journey via Hamburg, Leipzig, Plauen and Regensburg took almost three weeks. It was made all the worse by the difficulty they had in finding suitable accommodation, and by constant squabbling between Rumford and his daughter. The one bright spot for Sarah was a day at the Leipzig Fair, and for Rumford a night he was able to spend with an old flame, Baroness de Kalb.

When they arrived in Munich, Rumford found that many of his old enemies were still in powerful positions, and that the country was being ruled by a regency council of which he was not a member. Carl Theodore fled from the city on 2 August to Lokwitz in Saxony, so that for the time being Rumford was left with nothing to do, and it was only by chance that he was brought back into power with a vengeance. Count Morawitzky, the Bavarian army commander, had exercised his right to close the gates of the city of Munich to prevent the Austrian General La Tour passing his army through. The general was sorely offended by this action and, when he demanded redress, the disagreement was resolved by the regency council relieving Morawitzky of his command and replacing him with Rumford. Some thought that this was done on the grounds that it might be wiser to appoint a foreigner to take the blame if, as seemed likely, the Bavarian army was defeated.

Be that as it may, Rumford, something of an amateur soldier, who had never fought a battle in his life, was charged with defending Munich. It was a tough assignment. The gates of the city were closed and there were 12,000 Bavarian troops inside them, together with all the civilians, and Rumford had to use all his experience, ingenuity and inventiveness simply to feed them all. His strategy in dealing with the Austrians and the French was to remain strictly neutral and play off one against the other and to hope for the best. First, he persuaded the Austrians to camp outside the city by apologizing to General La Tour for his predecessor's actions, and by assuring him that he would fight the French if they were to attack Munich. Then he called on the French commander, General Moreau, to explain that there would be no point in the French attacking the city because he had already prevented the Austrians from entering it.

This policy paid off and events began to move in Rumford's favour. The French established a small post close to the English Garden between 29 August and 11 September, but they withdrew when shelled by the Austrians. Thereafter, following the defeat of another French army under General Jourdan further to the south, General Moreau had to move his troops away from Munich, and this led to the Austrians pulling back to Vienna. Rumford had defended Munich without a drop of blood being shed, and he became a national hero overnight. A monument, which is still there today, was erected in the English Garden to commemorate his achievement; a street was renamed *Rumfordstrasse*; Sarah, who had actually contributed very little, became Countess Sarah Rumford and was granted a pension of £200 for life in her own right; and when Carl Theodore returned to the city on 7 October, he appointed Rumford as Head of the Police Department.

As life in Munich returned to normal in the autumn of 1796, the atmosphere was one of great relief and much joy, in which both Rumford and Sarah revelled. He lived in

Rumfordstrasse street sign in Munich. (Photo by Karin Oakley)

great style with two aides-de-camp, Captain Count Taxis and Lieutenant Spreti, a valet, a groom, an ostler, a personal doctor and hordes of lesser servants. Although being head of the police involved him in tiresome day-to-day activities of civil affairs he still had time for other things, and he once again began to consider his future.

Before returning to Munich, his thoughts had been turning in the direction of furthering his scientific career, and now they moved that way again. In particular, he extended the research he had begun during his first stay in England on measuring the explosive force of gunpowder and published his results in a paper to the Royal Society on

4 May 1797. He also carried out his most famous series of experiments on boring cannon. 'Whilst superintending the boring of cannons in the workshops of the military arsenal in Munich,' he wrote, 'I was struck with the very considerable degree of Heat which a brass gun acquires in a short time in being bored'[13] and he saw in this a suitable topic for research. His reputation as a scientist rests mainly on this work.

Rumford also used his time to write more essays, mainly concerned with the propagation of heat in fluids, which was an extension of his earlier work on measuring the thermal conductivity of materials, and to popularize his existing collection. Never one to miss any chance of self-aggrandizement, he sent copies to the King and Queen of England, to George Washington, to Catherine the Great, Empress of Russia, and to many other international worthies. He also managed to get his essays published in French by Professor Pictet, who became a great supporter and friend, and in German through the husband of Baroness de Kalbe.

But life for Rumford was never all work and no play. While carrying out these experiments he found the time for other more social pursuits. In August he spent eight days in Berchtesgaden and Salzburg with Princess Taxis, the wife of his aide-de-camp; he tried to persuade Lady Palmerston to come to live with him during the winter months; and in July he went on a touring holiday with Sarah.

Sarah was, in fact, much happier in Munich than she had been in England, and she found both the weather and the way of life more to her liking. Life in the court circles in which she spent most of her time was controlled by the seventeen-year-old wife of the Elector, who was now seventy-one. The reversal of the numbers in their ages caused much comment and was matched by their completely different temperaments – the old introvert and the young extrovert not seemingly having much in common. There was a never-ending round of balls and parties and various goings-on at a château that Rumford owned on the shores of Lake Starnberger at Berg. Her father, moreover, seemed to be more pleased with Sarah; he even wrote to Loammi Baldwin that 'she is the comfort of my life, a very good girl, much loved here by everybody who knows her';[14] and he gave her a white shaggy dog called Cora as a present.

Such sentiments did not, alas, last long. Rumford still thought that his daughter's education was sadly lacking and he tried to arrange lessons for her in French, Italian, drawing and music, but Sarah would have none of it. She was, in fact, very much engaged because she had forged a relationship with Count Taxis. He came from a fine German family, well known to Rumford, and one would have thought he might have been regarded as a very suitable son-in-law. Instead, when he asked, via Countess Nogarola, for Sarah's hand in marriage, both he and his regiment were ordered to leave Munich immediately.

Sarah might just have been prepared to forgive her father, even though Taxis was the second suitor that he had sent packing unceremoniously. She was not, however,

Count Rumford's signature and seal with the signatures of Countess Nogarola and Sarah
Rumford as witnesses.

prepared to be very forgiving when she discovered by
chance that she had an illegitimate half-sister. It was a
particularly cruel blow, and the circumstances in which it
came to light made it even more so. Sarah, helped by
Countess Nogarola, had spent much time in preparing a
forty-fourth birthday party for her father on 26 March
1797. There were songs by the Countess's children, play-
acting by a group of children from a local workhouse, and
even an attempt at a speech in Italian from Sarah. But all
Rumford's attention seemed to be centred on a little girl
called Sophy Baumgarten, and when Sarah asked the reason
for this she was told the truth by Countess Nogarola, whose
sister was the girl's mother. Sarah wrote that 'the striking

resemblance that existed between my father and the said Sophy put it beyond a doubt that I was no longer to consider myself an only child. . . . My surprise and vexation were great, and, had I been alone, most likely vent would have been given by a few tears'.[15] And when she tried to remonstrate with her father he simply scolded her for having an affair with Count Taxis. The father–daughter relationship was irrevocably damaged and all she could think of was 'retaliation, or, in other less soft words, revenge'[16] but, so far as is known, she never converted her thoughts into action.

There was, also, another unexpected spin-off from the birthday party. Rumford had been touched by the performance of the children from the workhouse and, wanting to commemorate the scene, he wrote to Loammi Baldwin offering to present the town of Concord with $2,000 worth of 3 per cent US Government Stock, so that the interest from it could be used to clothe six boys and six girls from poor homes each year on Sarah's birthday. The selectmen of Concord who had to decide the issue finally agreed to accept the offer of money, but did not fully implement the terms of the bequest. This, in fact, was not done until Sarah's death fifty-four years later.

Although the main reason for Rumford's charitable gift was emotional, it also reflected his continuing dream of one day returning to America. And that dream must have been resurrected by the uncertainty surrounding his future. He was still a national hero to some Bavarians but much of the old antagonism towards him was again rearing its ugly head.

There were suggestions that he was corruptly pocketing money from the military, police and workhouse jobs with which he was, or had been, involved. And the row he had had with the Munich City Council over the English Garden blew up again. Before leaving for London in 1795, he had drawn up plans to build a broad promenade right around the city, but the scheme was not supported by the council and, while Rumford was away in London, they constructed a number of buildings on the proposed route of the promenade which would effectively prevent it from ever being constructed. Rumford, however, was to have the last laugh, as he commonly did. While organizing the defence of the city, he had all the new council buildings removed on the grounds that it was militarily necessary for the sites they occupied to be vacant to give better visibility.

Rumford's position was also being undermined because the Austrians had become suspicious of him following a proposal he had put forward after the siege of Munich to increase the strength of the Bavarian army to 26,000 so that Bavaria could be less dependent on Austria. This almost led to war between the two countries and Carl Theodore had to sack many of the people involved in the plan to pacify the Austrian emperor. Rumford survived but as time went by it became clear both to him and to Carl Theodore that his position was becoming more and more untenable. It was a matter, then, of devising some way of letting him leave the country with dignity, and the clever solution that emerged was for Theodore to appoint Rumford as his Minister Plenipotentiary to the Court of St James in England. It may well have been Rumford's own idea and he was well pleased with it, thinking that he would be well received in London where he would be able to maintain his lifestyle, engage in some official functions and pursue his interests at the heart of the world's leading scientific nation. So for the second time he packed up and, together with Sarah and his entourage, arrived in London on 19 September 1798.

On his last arrival in London he had been robbed. This time he was in for an even greater surprise.

THE NATURE OF HEAT

Rumford is best remembered today as a scientist, and he published over seventy papers in his lifetime. He had a particular interest in the nature of heat, which he attributed to his reading, when he was only sixteen years old, a long chapter on 'Fire' in the book *New Method of Chemistry*, written by Hermann Boerhaave, a Dutch physician, botanist and chemist. Later, Rumford wrote that 'to engage in experiments on heat was always one of my most agreeable employments. I was often prevented by other matters from devoting my attention to it, but whenever I could snatch a moment I returned to it with increased interest.'[1] And on 8 November 1797 he wrote 'I can conceive of no delight like that of detecting and calling forth into action the hidden forces of nature.'[2]

This is exactly what he did in his most famous series of experiments which he carried out in the arsenal in Munich during 1797, investigating the amount of heat produced during the boring of a cannon. His observations, reported to the Royal Society on 25 January 1798 in a paper entitled 'An Experimental Inquiry Concerning the Source of Heat Which is Excited by Friction', and published as his Essay IX, made a significant contribution to the on-going, but inconclusive, discussion as to the nature of heat.

Everyone knows whether they feel hot or cold, but very few can give coherent answers to the questions 'What is heat?' or 'What is cold?' They are difficult questions to answer in simple language even today, and they were certainly tough in earlier times. But there were similar enquiries as to the nature of light, fire, electricity, magnetism and gravity. The lack of clear-cut answers, and the fact that many of the ideas propounded seem to modern eyes to have come from never-never land, simply reflected the confused state of scientific and technological understanding at the time.

So far as heat was concerned there were, in Rumford's day, two theories. The first, nowadays called the kinetic theory, probably originated from the well-known fact that a solid can be heated by friction or by hammering. The basic idea was that the heat of a body was associated with the constant movement of the particles of which the body was made. Frictional rubbing or hammering of a solid increased this movement so that the body got hotter. Francis Bacon (1561–1626), an early exponent of this theory, wrote: 'heat itself, its essence and quiddity is motion and nothing else . . . not uniformly of the whole body, but in the smaller parts of it. . . . so that the body acquires a motion alternative, perpetually quivering, striving, and struggling . . . whence springs the fury of heat'.[3] John Locke (1632–1704) put it another way: 'heat is a very brisk agitation of the insensible parts of the object, which produces in us that sensation from which we denominate the body hot; so what in our sensation is heat, in the object is nothing but motion'.[4] And Robert Hooke (1635–1703) described heat as 'nothing else but a brisk and vehement agitation of the parts of a body'.[5]

The kinetic theory was also accepted by Robert Boyle (1627–91), Isaac Newton (1642–1727), Gottfried Leibniz (1646–1716), Henry Cavendish (1731–1810), Thomas Young (1773–1829) and Humphry Davy (1778–1829), but an alternative – the caloric theory – came to the fore in the latter part of the eighteenth century. It owed much of its popularity to Antoine Lavoisier (1743–94), sometimes referred to as the father of modern chemistry, and was supported by Joseph Black (1728–99), the Marquis de Laplace (1749–1827), John Dalton (1766–1844), John Leslie (1766–1832), Claude Berthollet (1748–1822) and Johan Berzelius (1779–1848).

The caloric theory supposed that heat was a mysterious fluid which somehow flowed into a body when it was heated and flowed out when it was cooled. The hotter a body became the more caloric it contained, which explained why its volume increased. Lavoisier regarded caloric as a real substance and even included it, along with light, in his table of thirty-three chemical elements which he produced in 1789. However, because there was no evidence for an increase in weight as a body got hotter the caloric had to be regarded as weightless. To account for other facts it was also necessary to assume that the particles within a substance were surrounded by caloric, which they attracted, but that the caloric was self-repellant. Dalton summarized it in 1808 when he wrote, 'the most probable

TABLE OF SIMPLE SUBSTANCES.

Simple ſubſtances belonging to all the kingdoms of na-ture, which may be conſidered as the elements of bo-dies.

New Names.				*Correſpondent old Names.*
Light	-	-	-	Light.
Caloric	-	-	-	{ Heat. Principle or element of heat. Fire. Igneous fluid. Matter of fire and of heat.
Oxygen	-	-	-	{ Dephlogiſticated air. Empyreal air. Vital air, or Baſe of vital air.
Azote	-	-	-	{ Phlogiſticated air or gas. Mephitis, or its baſe.
Hydrogen	-		-	{ Inflammable air or gas, or the baſe of inflammable air.

Oxydable and Acidifiable ſimple Subſtances not Metallic.

New Names.				*Correſpondent old names.*
Sulphur	-	-	-	}
Phoſphorus	-	-	-	} The ſame names.
Charcoal	-	-	-	}
Muriatic radical	-			}
Fluoric radical	-		-	} Still unknown.
Boracic radical	-		-	}

Oxydable and Acidifiable ſimple Metallic Bodies.

Part of Lavoisier's old list of elements in his *Traité Élémentaire de Chimie* (1789).
It demonstrates the confused state of understanding at the time.

opinion concerning the nature of heat is that of its being an elastic fluid of great subtility, the particles of which repel one another, but are attracted by other bodies'.[6] With hindsight it was clearly a case of

> All philosophers who find
> A favourite system to their mind,
> In every point, to make it fit,
> Will force all nature to submit.[7]

Historically, it was Count Rumford who first provided the major clue which enabled a sensible decision to be made about which of the two rival theories was correct, but before he could do so a clearer understanding of temperature and of an associated concept, the quantity of heat, had to be developed.

As early as 1592 Galileo had made a thermometer for measuring temperature which depended on the expansion of air when it was heated. Modern thermometers in contrast make use of the expansion of liquids. The German physicist G.D. Fahrenheit made one in 1701 which had alcohol in a bulb at one end of a thin uniform tube which was evacuated and sealed at the other end. The alcohol level moved up and down the tube as the temperature changed. Fahrenheit replaced the alcohol with mercury in 1714, and the Swedish astronomer, Anders Celsius, made a similar thermometer in 1742. Their thermometers were graduated with different scales which subsequently became known as the Fahrenheit and Centigrade (or Celsius) scales. Celsius took the freezing point of water (0°C) as his zero and the boiling point of water (100°C) as his upper fixed point. Earlier, Fahrenheit, in order to avoid negative readings of air temperatures, had taken his zero (0°F) as the temperature of a mixture of salt with ice, and his upper fixed point (100°F) as an approximation to normal body temperature. This meant that the freezing point of water was 32°F on his scale and the boiling point was 180 degrees higher at 212°F.

The temperature of a body, however, although it indicates how hot it is, gives no measure of the quantity of heat that it contains. This was first measured by the Scottish chemist Joseph Black, who demonstrated in the 1760s that it depended on the temperature and the weight of the body, and *on what it was made of*. To measure the quantities of heat concerned, Black used the British Thermal Unit (BThU), defined as the quantity of heat required to raise the temperature of 1 pound of water by 1°F but that unit was later replaced by the calorie (cal), the heat required to raise the temperature of 1 gram of water by 1°C. As this is a very small amount of heat, the kilocalorie (kcal), equal to 1000 cal, is commonly used.

To raise the temperature of 10 grams of water by 1°C, or 1 gram by 10°C, requires 10 calories, and so on. In summary, the number of calories is equal to the weight in grams multiplied by the rise in temperature in degrees Centigrade. But this is only true for water and Black showed that every different material had its own specific heat capacity, defined as the number of calories required to raise the temperature of 1 gram of the material by 1°C. The specific heat capacity of water, on this basis, is 1 calorie per gram per °C. For copper, in the same units, it is 0.09, for iron 0.11, and for alcohol 0.59.

Since his reading of Boerhaave's *New Method of Chemistry*, Rumford had been brought up to believe in the kinetic theory rather than the caloric theory. It is not surprising, then, that he recognized a chance to contribute to the debate when he observed the large amount of heat produced in a short time during the boring of cannons in the Munich arsenal. In 1797 he had written to Pictet that, 'I have hitherto taken particular care cautiously to avoid bewildering myself in those abstruse speculations.'[8] But the next year he wrote, 'The more I meditated on these phenomena, the more they appeared to be curious and interesting. A thorough investigation of them seemed even to bid fair to give a farther insight into the given nature of Heat; and to enable us to form some reasonable conjecture, respecting the existence, or non-existence, of an *igneous* fluid – a subject on which the opinions of philosophers have, in all ages, been much divided.'[9] And by 1804 he was bold enough to write, 'I think I shall live to drive *caloric* off the stage.'[10]

In his first series of experiments, he used the body of an unbored, 6-pounder cannon made of brass. This consisted of a solid cylinder that had been cast vertically and was 60 cm longer than the cannon which would be made from it, to prevent excessive strains building up as the brass cooled. The extra length was normally cut off when the cannon was made, and it was the piece used by Rumford for his experiments. He cut and machined it so that it formed a cylinder 25 cm long and 20 cm in diameter, which was attached to what would normally have become the muzzle of the cannon by a small neck of metal 9 cm long and 6 cm in diameter. He then mounted the whole horizontally in a lathe, which was operated through a system of gears, driven by two horses walking round in a circle in an adjacent room. With a sharp horizontal borer he made a cylindrical hole 18 cm long and 9 cm in diameter. He then fitted a flat, blunt piece of hardened steel, 16 mm thick, 10 cm long and nearly 9 cm wide, into this cylindrical hole, pressed very tightly against the base by a spring. He also drilled a smaller hole sideways into the main portion of the remaining brass into which a thermometer was fitted, and encased the whole, as far as possible, with thick flannel to minimize heat loss.

All was now ready for the test. Keeping the blunt piece of steel stationary, he used the horses to turn the cannon in the lathe. After 960 revolutions, taking about 30 minutes, the temperature recorded on the thermometer had risen from 15°C to 55°C. On cutting the hollow cylinder away from the main part of the cannon he measured its weight as 51 kg, and found that the weight of the abraded metal was 54 g, only 1/944th part of the original weight. To counter suggestions that some of the heat might have come from the surrounding air, Rumford repeated his experiment with the open end of the hollow cylinder closed by a piston so that no air could enter. He found that it made no difference to the measurements he had previously made.

Rumford estimated that about 230 kcal of heat had been produced, which would have been able to boil 2.3 kg of ice-cold water, but to measure this more accurately he adapted

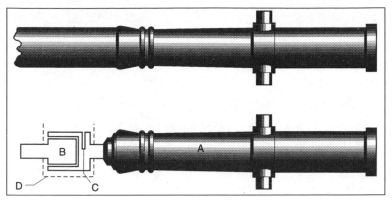

Diagram of Rumford's cannon-boring equipment. Top: original casting of cannon body; bottom: machined cannon set up for experiment. A. Main cannon body which is rotated. B. Stationary blunt piece of hard steel. C. Hole for thermometer. D. Box containing water.

his apparatus by fitting a box, made of deal, around the hollow cylinder. The holes in the sides were made watertight by fitting oiled leather collars, and enough water, at 15°C, was added to the box to surround the cylinder completely. It was then rotated at about 32 revolutions per minute. After 60 minutes the temperature of the water had risen to 42°C; after 90 minutes to 61°C; after 120 to 81°C; and after 150 minutes the water actually boiled. As there had been 8.5 kg of water, at least 730 kcal of heat must have been produced, but in fact much more heat was produced because it wasn't only the water that got hot.

Rumford wrote that 'the result of this beautiful experiment was very striking and the pleasure it afforded me amply repaid me for all the trouble I had had in contriving and arranging the complicated machinery used in making it'.[11] The experiment had a similar effect on others. 'It would be difficult to describe', Rumford wrote, 'the surprise and astonishment expressed in the countenances of the bystanders, on seeing so large a quantity of cold water heated, and actually made to boil, without any fire.'[12]

Rumford was at pains to point out that his experiment could be repeated over and over again with the same cannon body; that the same large quantities of heat could be regenerated over and over again; and that the larger piece of the cannon body could still be bored in the usual way to make a normal cannon when he had finished with it. But what had impressed him most was the seemingly inexhaustible quantity of heat that had been produced. Whence had it come and what was it? He concluded that it had come from the frictional forces involved and that 'it appears to me to be extremely difficult, if not quite impossible, to form any distinct idea of anything capable of being excited and communicated in the manner the Heat was excited and communicated in these experiments, except it be MOTION'.[13] The Irishman John Tyndall, who succeeded Michael Faraday at the Royal Institution in 1854, wrote in 1871, 'Hardly anything more powerful against the materiality of heat has been since adduced, hardly anything conclusive in the way of establishing that heat is what Rumford considered it to be, Motion.'[14]

With two horses involved, Rumford's experiment could hardly be described as a laboratory experiment, but later he developed a smaller-scale version. This consisted of an apparatus in which the abutting, flat surfaces of two brass hemispheres, 9 cm in diameter and both immersed in water in a 30 cm globe, could be rubbed against each other by rotating the upper one. The amount of heat produced could be calculated by measuring the rise in temperature of the water. Contemporaneously, in 1799 Humphry Davy was using a clockwork mechanism to rub together two pieces of ice,

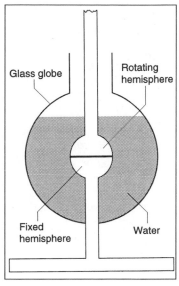

Rumford's frictional heat experiment. The upper, brass hemisphere is rotated over the lower fixed one.

15 cm long, 5 cm wide and 17 mm thick, in a vacuum, in a surrounding atmosphere at $-1.5°C$. He found that the two pieces of ice were almost completely converted into water at $1.5°C$ within a few minutes. He concluded, in keeping with the idea of the kinetic theory, that heat 'may be defined as a peculiar motion, probably a vibration of the corpuscles of a body tending to separate them'.[15]

Meanwhile Rumford was carrying out his second series of experiments designed to discover whether or not heat weighed anything. If it consisted of a fluid, such as caloric, it might be expected to weigh something. If it was simply a vibration, it would be weightless. He made three bottles, as identical as possible, and filled them with equal weights of water, mercury and alcohol. The bottles were then hermetically sealed and stored in a room in which the temperature was maintained as close to 16°C as possible for more than twenty-four hours. The bottles were then weighed, using a balance belonging to Carl Theodore which was claimed to be accurate to one part in a million, and the three weights were exactly balanced by tying lengths of silver wire round the necks of the lighter bottles. They were then moved, for forty-eight hours, into a room maintained at a temperature of −1°C. The water froze in its bottle but, though each of the three liquids must have lost different amounts of heat, the weights of the bottles had not changed. Nor did they change when restored to the warmer room. Rumford boldly concluded that 'all attempts to discover any effect of heat upon the apparent weight of bodies will be fruitless'[16] and regarded his experimental results as a body blow to the caloric theory.

A third series of experiments carried out by Rumford involved the miscibility of liquids. If liquids were made up of particles each surrounded by an 'atmosphere' of caloric, which repelled other caloric, it was not easy to see why two liquids should mix. On the other hand, if the liquids contained vibrating particles they could readily mix with each other. Rumford devised a particularly striking way of carrying out this experiment. He put some water in a tall cylindrical vessel and, through a tube, carefully poured in some saturated salt solution, which has a higher density than water, to form a lower layer. He then added a single drop of black oil of cloves, which sank through the water but floated on top of the salt solution. As the two liquids slowly mixed, despite the higher density of the salt solution, the drop of oil rose steadily until it floated right on the top.

Having satisfied himself about the general nature of heat, Rumford turned his attention to the possible relationship between the amount of heat produced in his cannon boring experiment and the amount of energy expanded (i.e., the amount of work done) by the horses. What he found, using modern units, was that 1 calorie of heat was produced by 5.60 joule of energy, where 1 joule is the energy needed to raise 102 g (the weight of a small apple) 1 m. This value, of what came to be called the mechanical equivalent of heat, was of great historical value, even though it was very inaccurate compared with today's accepted value of 4.184 joule per calorie. Its importance lay in the quantitative connection it made between energy and heat. As one joule (1 J) is only a very small amount of energy, the kilojoule (1 kJ), equal to 1000 joule, is more commonly used; 4.184 kJ of energy will provide 1 kcal. Knowing this value enables all sorts of calculations to be easily made. For example, 15 kJ of energy are required to make a small cup of hot coffee. The energy, it is now known, can be provided by a fire, by electricity, by gas, by a microwave cooker or, given time, by repeated vigorous stirring. On a different level, it also became possible to calculate the theoretical weight of water that could be pumped by a steam engine to a given height using the heat available from 1 kg of coal.

Rumford's value for the mechanical equivalent of heat was inaccurate and he did not fully understand its

Julius Robert von Mayer.

significance, but obtaining a value at all as early as 1798 was his most outstanding single achievement. It was more than forty years before any further advance was made through the work of the German Julius Robert von Mayer and the Englishman James Prescott Joule.

Mayer, the son of an apothecary, was born in Heilbronn in 1814. He studied medicine at Tübingen University and, despite being expelled in 1837 for belonging to a secret student society, qualified a year later. In 1840 he was appointed as the ship's doctor on the three-masted *Java*, which set off on a year-long journey to the Far East. There were twenty-eight crew and no passengers so he had plenty of time for reading and thinking. He wrote that 'he enjoyed a harmless peace of mind, which disposed him by preference to scientific occupation',[17] and he began to consider the production of heat in living organisms. At Surabaya, when several of the crew had to be bled because they were ill, he found that their venous blood was much redder than he had anticipated. The locals told him that this was due to the smaller amount of oxygen required to maintain body temperature in the tropics. He began to wonder what happened to the total amount of energy available from a person's food. Some of it, he concluded, must be converted into heat and some into work such as muscular movement. This was the unlikely beginning of what came to be known as the conservation of energy.

When he got back home he started to study physics so that he could develop his embryonic ideas, and he was the first person to realize that there were in fact many different forms of energy. There was *potential* energy, he said, due to the position of an object; water at the top of a waterfall had potential energy, for example, because it could do work as it fell down. *Kinetic* energy was due to motion, as in an express train or in molecular motion. *Heat* energy could heat something up or operate a steam engine. *Electrical* energy could bring about chemical decomposition or run a motor. And *chemical* energy was apparent when coal or oil was burnt to produce heat. Mayer's idea was that there was only a fixed amount of energy involved in any particular process. It could be changed from one form to another, but the total amount could be neither increased nor decreased. Energy was always conserved. It could be neither created nor destroyed, but only transformed.

Following Rumford, he obtained more accurate values for the mechanical equivalent of heat by measuring the rise in temperature of pulp in a paper factory when it was stirred by an amount of energy equal to five horse-power. He also calculated a value, 3.58 joule per calorie, by assuming that all the work done in compressing a volume of air was converted into heat.

Mayer, like Rumford before him, was not an established scientist and he came up against terrible difficulties when he tried to get his work published. His first paper, submitted to the *Annalen der Physick und Chemie* was pigeon-holed by its editor, Johann Poggendorff, without even an acknowledgement, and two later papers, published in Justus von Liebig's *Annalen der Chemie und Pharmazie* in 1842 and 1845 roused unexpected hostility among other scientists who looked upon him as an interloper and found his views rather hard to stomach or not original. Some even accused him of being a megalomaniac.

The effect of this on Mayer, a married man with a kind and trusting nature, and a well-respected doctor in his home town, was disastrous. One sunny morning in May 1850, after a sleepless night, he flung himself out of a high window. He escaped with serious leg injuries but remained so depressed that he had to resort to periods of treatment in an asylum during the 1850s. Some reports actually said that he had died there in 1878, but they were untrue. What actually happened was that John Tyndall and two Germans, Hermann von Helmholtz and Rudolf Clausius, came to support Mayer very strongly, so that he did achieve some recognition in his later years. He was awarded the Copley medal by the Royal Society in 1871.

The work he had begun was carried on by the Englishman James Prescott Joule, who was born in 1818 near Manchester, the son of a wealthy brewer. He was educated, along with his brother, at home, with John Dalton as one of his tutors, and when he was only twenty years old he began his researches in a laboratory provided by his father next to the brewery. Later in life, he actually ran the brewery while continuing his research and he was wealthy enough to continue to do this for some time without needing to occupy any academic position. When his funds did run out, in 1878, he was granted a pension by Queen Victoria.

James Prescott Joule.

Joule expanded the scope of Rumford's and Mayer's measurements of the mechanical equivalent of heat and improved on their accuracy. First, he measured the rise in temperature of some water when a small electromagnet, immersed in the water, was rotated between the poles of another magnet. Secondly, he measured the rise in temperature when water was forced through capillary tubes; thirdly, the rise in temperature when air was compressed; and fourthly, the rise in temperature when some paddles were rotated in water or oil or mercury by a system of falling weights. In the final report of his work, *On the Mechanical Equivalent of Heat*, presented before the Royal Society in 1849, he concluded that its value was 4.154 joule per calorie.

Joule's name has been commemorated by its adoption as the unit of energy and therefore heat in the SI system (Système International d'Unités) which came into use in the 1960s. And as heat is now recognized as just one of the various forms of energy, the joule has largely replaced the calorie as the unit of heat. 1 J is equivalent to 0.239 calorie, or 1 calorie to 4.184 joule. One of the consequences, in everyday life, is that both units are widely used on most food packaging to indicate the energy content of the food. Typical figures, per 100 gram of food, are 30 kj (7.2 kcal) for sliced beans; 172 (65) for milk; 1065 (255) for chips; and 1680 (402) for sugar. Typical energy requirements, per day, are 4184 kJ (1,000 kcal) for a baby, rising to 20,000 (4780) for a manual labourer. It all seems very remote from a cannon in the arsenal in Munich.

Joule paid a handsome tribute to Rumford's work and very few argued with John Tyndall's considered judgement when he wrote in 1880: 'When the history of the dynamical theory of heat is completely written, the man, who in opposition to the scientific belief of his time, could experiment, and reason upon experiment, as Rumford did, may count on a foremost place.'[18]

THE INGENIOUS INVENTOR

Count Rumford was an ingenious inventor as well as a successful scientist and his inventions were particularly practical and useful. They were mainly in the field of lighting, heating and cooking, and many of them originated in his early attempts to make the living conditions in the workhouses he had established as good and efficient and economical as he could. The methods in general use were unsatisfactory on almost any count.

Eighteenth-century lighting, providing only a gloomy and depressing environment, depended on candles or oil lamps which had been in use for many years. The candles were made of tallow or other animal fats, spermaceti or beeswax, but they were smoky and expensive and gave only a flickering light which was inconsistent unless the wick was kept trimmed. Oil lamps consisted of a flat wick, at first made from vegetable fibres but later woven, dipping into an oil such as linseed oil, rape-seed oil, whale oil, olive oil or colza oil (from the root of the swede), which was burnt at the top of the wick. They gave a steadier and a brighter light than candles, but the brightness of the flame, as in candles, depended very much on the state of the wick.

The Argand lamp, invented in 1780 by the Swiss chemist Ami Argand, was particularly successful. It was manufactured in England by Matthew Boulton, James Watt's associate, and in France under the name of the Quinquet lamp. It gave an improved light by using a tubular wick surrounding a hollow metal cylinder instead of the standard flat wick. Air passing up the hollow cylinder came out at the top into the centre of the flame, enabling it to burn more brightly. The flame was also surrounded by a cylindrical glass container. Argand lamps were quite expensive but did give out much more light, and made it much easier to read at night.

Rumford realized that he needed some method of measuring light intensity if he was to compare one lamp with another. 'Being employed', he wrote, 'in making a number of experiments to determine if possible the most economical method of lighting up a very large workhouse . . . a method occurred to me for measuring the relative quantities of light emitted by lamps of different construction, candles, etc.'[1] And so it was that he made what he called a photometer in 1794. He used the principle adopted by the Frenchman J.H. Lambert in 1760, but there is no evidence that Rumford knew of Lambert's work at the time.

Rumford's photometer depended on comparing the shadows cast by two different sources of light, and on the known fact that the intensity of light diminished in proportion as the square of the distance from the source increased. That meant that the intensity of light was four times less when twice the distance away from the source, and nine times less when three times the distance away. The

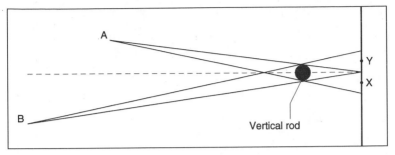

The principle of Rumford's photometer.

principle of the photometer is explained in the diagram above. The two light sources, A and B, are moved in or out until the two shadows that they cast on the screen match. Then

$$\frac{\text{Brightness of source A}}{\text{Brightness of source B}} = \frac{(\text{Distance AX})^2}{(\text{Distance BY})^2}$$

In Rumford's final design of photometer he had two vertical rods 75 mm apart and 50 mm in front of a white screen at the back of a black box. The light sources were placed on carriages that could be moved by winches along platforms, one 3.5 m and the other 6 m long. With this equipment Rumford was able to amass a lot of significant data. He found, for example, that the light from an Argand lamp was nine times cheaper than that from wax candles; that there was a loss of about 15 per cent of light when it passed through clean glass; and that there was a loss of about 30 per cent when light was reflected from even the best mirror. He also introduced the idea of candle power as the intensity of light emanating from a candle made to a particular specification. This was used for over a century as an international standard unit, and light intensity was expressed in terms of candle-power until the introduction of the candela unit in 1948.

Rumford used his photometer to compare one lamp, or one fuel, with another, and this eventually led him to design improved lamps that came to be known as Rumford lamps or, because he did not want them to be associated with existing designs, as Rumford illuminators; they were first described at a meeting of the *Institut National de France* in March 1806. The lamps had three new features. First, they used more than one wick, either flat or of the cylindrical Argand type, placed close together side-by-side. This was intended to keep each flame as hot as possible for as long as possible, because the hotter the flame the brighter the light. Rumford found in fact that one of his new lamps with four flat wicks placed 5 mm apart would give more light than six Argand lamps.

Secondly, the oil reservoir was redesigned and repositioned to improve the flow of oil through the wick. In a standard Argand lamp the oil was sucked up into the wick from a container below it. With existing oils, this took place satisfactorily when the container was full but less and less well as the oil level fell. Rumford stored the oil in a circular hollow tube passing round the circumference of the lamp at the height of the top of the wick. This positioning also allowed more light to pass downwards if the lamp was hung from a ceiling.

Thirdly, he used ground-glass covers or lampshades made of silk or white gauze to diffuse the light from his lamps, following a well-established Chinese practice. This produced a softer light than a standard Argand lamp, without any great loss in efficiency, and the shades could also be designed to cover some of the uglier parts of the lamp. He linked his concern with the quality of light to his interest in the opposite sex by writing that 'no decayed beauty ought ever to expose her face to the direct rays of an Argand lamp', and 'that mysterious light which comes from bodies moderately illuminated is certainly most favourable to female beauty'.[2]

The Argand lamp had been patented in England in 1784 but Rumford never took out any patents to cover his ideas. He wrote, 'I desire only that the whole world should profit by it, without preventing others from using it with equal freedom.'[3] Nevertheless, he brought a lawsuit against two French lamp-makers, Bordier and Pallebot, claiming that lamps they began to make in 1809 were based on his design. The case was heard in 1812 and Rumford was well satisfied when the judgement went in his favour.

He collected together all his work on lighting in a book *Of the Management of Light in Illumination*, published in 1812. He wrote: 'I shall have done much if I succeed in turning the attention of ingenious men to this interesting subject; and I sincerely hope that the improvements resulting from their united efforts will soon cause all those I have proposed to be forgotten.'[4] Within the next few years the introduction of gas, electricity and paraffin or kerosene for lighting purposes had turned his hope into reality.

Rumford was as keen on heating buildings as he was on lighting them and he extended his interest in the theory of heat into the very practical area of keeping people warm. As with lighting, the existing methods were rather primitive. The earliest Stone Age buildings of which any traces remain are 'houses' made of mammoth bones, notably those around Mezhirich, near Kiev. It appears that they were heated by a wood or peat fire burning in a hearth in the centre of the floor. The smoke, it was hoped, would pass out through a covered hole in the centre of the roof, which was made of hides stretched over a bone framework.

Simple chimneys were first mentioned in the early fourth century BC by Theophrastus, a pupil of Aristotle, but they only became common in the twelfth century AD in the cold climate of Europe. With these, the fire was situated against an outside wall and a hood was used to collect the smoke and channel it up through the wall into a chimney protruding from the roof.

Such open fires, still very attractive today, were strongly criticized by Rumford. In his essay 'Of Chimney Fireplaces, with Proposals for Improving them to Save Fuel, to Render Dwelling Houses more Comfortable and Salubrious, and Effectively to Prevent Chimneys from Smoking' in 1796, he wrote, 'those cold and chilling draughts of air on one side of the body while the other is scorched by a chimney fire . . . cannot but be highly detrimental to health, and in weak and delicate constitutions must often produce the most fatal effects'.[5] In the same essay he comments on the 'vast dark cloud which continually hangs over London'[6] and on its origin in 'the unconsumed coal, which, having stolen wings from the innumerable fires of this great city, has escaped by the chimneys, and continues to sail about in the air . . .'.[7] And in the 1797 essay 'Of the Management of Fire and the Economy of Fuel' he concludes that 'no less than seven-eighths of the heat generated, or which with proper management might be generated, from the fuel actually consumed is carried up into the atmosphere with the smoke, and totally lost.'[8]

Rumford's suggestions for improvements involved a complete redesign of both fireplace and chimney. In his opinion the existing arrangement in which the fire burnt in a large rectangular space, open at the front, with a straight vertical chimney coming out from the back at the top simply caused a great deal of turbulent flow in the chimney which resulted in a lot of disastrous down-draughts. He proposed three main changes. First, he rounded off and narrowed the entrance to the chimney at

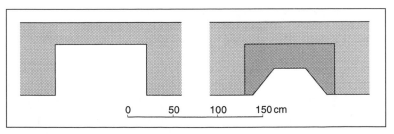

Views from the top of old (left) and new (right) fireplaces. The width of the fireplace was reduced from 125 cm to 80 and the depth from 75 cm to 36.

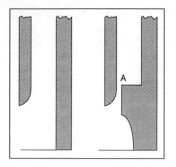

Side views of old (left) and new (right) chimneys. The throat of the new chimney, A, was narrowed to about 10 cm.

the bottom, which came to be called the throat, so that that it was only about 10 cm deep from back to front. This gave a much more streamlined flow of gases up the chimney. Secondly, he made the front opening of the fireplace smaller, reduced its depth, and inclined the sides inwards from front to back at an angle of 135° and the back inwards from top to bottom. This provided a quicker flow of air into the fireplace, and ensured as much radiation of heat as possible into the room from the sides and back. Thirdly, he introduced a register, now called a damper, so that the chimney could be fully closed when the fire was not burning or partially closed when more draught was required. This new design of fireplace, which was less smoky and gave out 50 to 66 per cent more heat than its predecessor, came to be called a Rumford stove and was much sought after by London society families. Lady Palmerston, Sir Joseph Banks, President of the Royal Society, Lady Templeton, the Earl of Bessborough and the Marquis of Salisbury were among the five hundred clients fitted with the new stoves. The stoves were also publicized through well-known cartoons by James Gillray and Isaac Cruikshank, and by poems written by Dr John Wolcot and published as *The Works of Peter Pindar* in 1802:

Cartoon of the Rumford stove by James Gillray (1757–1815).

Cartoon of the Rumford stove by George Cruickshank (1792–1878).

Lo, ev'ry parlour, drawing room I see,
Boasts of thy stoves and talks of naught but thee
Yet not alone my Lady and young Misses,
The Cooks themselves could smother thee with kisses.

Long as they chimneys shall thy praise endure:
Oblivion ne'er shall swallow Rumford's name,
Aloft ascending, lo, thy radiant Fame,
With thine own curling clouds of smoke shall rise
And sun-like give them lustre on the skies.

The stoves became so popular that Rumford found his name being used in advertisements for inferior products offered for sale by his competitors and to preserve his reputation he issued a general disclaimer. It said that, 'I feel it my duty to the public to declare that I am not the inventor of those stoves and grates that have been offered to the public for sale under my name.'[9] He had not, of course, patented any of his ideas and had indeed published details of how to construct the stoves so that anyone could benefit. He had also presented the Carron Company in Scotland with his patterns for a cast-iron grate so that they could produce it and sell it cheaply.

There was also some competition from across the Atlantic where Benjamin Franklin, an older contemporary of Rumford who had in fact been born within a few miles of him, had invented the Franklin or Pennsylvania stove around 1745 and had published a book, *Observations on the Cause and Cure of Smoky Chimneys*, in 1787. Franklin's stove was, however, significantly different from Rumford's; it had an enclosed fire within a box-like container made of cast iron.

Rumford's final experiment in room heating took him close to something like modern-day central heating. He published his ideas in 1804 in Essay XV, 'Of the Use of Steam as a Vehicle for Transporting Heat from One Place to Another', and he tried out the idea by heating the great lecture-room in the Royal Institution. 'The theatre', he wrote, 'is warmed in cold weather by steam, which, coming in covered and concealed tubes from the lower part of the house, circulates in a large semicircular copper tube 8 inches [20 cm] in diameter and above 60 feet [18 metres] long, which is concealed under the rising seats of the pit.'[10] The installation involved an arrangement for keeping the flow of steam separate from that of the condensed water, together with the fitting of expansion joints and safety valves, but there is no record of how successful it was or how long it lasted before it was closed down. Rumford clearly had some belief in it because he suggested its adoption for heating the hall of the *Institut National* in Paris, and in a variety of industrial processes. Benjamin Gott, the Mayor of Leeds in 1800, used steam from one boiler to heat a number of vats in his dye-works and he claimed that this reduced his heating costs by about 60 per cent. Some fellow dyers followed his example, but there was no great response because the technical difficulties were formidable.

Rumford did not, however, lose interest in heat. In 1812 he invented a calorimeter to use in comparing the heat provided by different fuels. It consisted of a container full of water with a long, coiled copper tube passing through it. The fuel under test was burnt at the entrance to this tube so that the heat from it raised the temperature of the water, which was measured with a thermometer with a specially long bulb. To minimize inaccuracies caused by heat loss to the atmosphere, he measured the weight of fuel required to raise the water from 5°C below room temperature to 5°C above it. In this way the heat lost to the atmosphere during the first half of the measurement is essentially regained during the second half. Rumford used this calorimeter to measure what came to be known as the heat of combustion of various types of wood, charcoal, tallow, peat and coal under different conditions. He also tested alcohol and ether – but the latter blew up and almost set his house on fire.

All these inventions were extremely innovative 200 years ago but it is Rumford's work on chimneys that has lasted longest because the basic principles he laid down are still widely used today. Happily it is no longer necessary to fit the removable slab he had to include to provide access for the unfortunate boy chimney sweeps.

On top of all the improvements that Rumford suggested in lighting and heating he can also claim to have revolutionized ideas on nutrition and cooking. His proposals in these fields were summarized in his essays 'Of Food; and Particularly of Feeding the Poor', written in 1796; 'Of the Management of Fire and the Economy of Fuel', written in 1797; and 'On the Construction of Kitchen Fire-places and Kitchen Utensils; together with Remarks and Observations Relating to the Various Processes of Cookery, and Proposals for Improving that Most Useful Art', written in 1799 and 1800.

A quote from the first essay – 'it seems to me to be more than probable that the number of inhabitants who may be supported in any country upon its internal produce depends almost as much upon the state of the art of cookery as upon agriculture'[11] – had a particularly marked effect because it was published at a time of high corn prices and general scarcity, which forced the British government to examine plans for dealing with a possible famine. Rumford's suggestions on how to handle the situation were commended by William Wilberforce, the anti-slavery campaigner, during a parliamentary debate on the Corn and Bread Bill in 1800.

The existing methods of cooking food over an open fire were uncontrollable and inefficient, and the fire cooked the cook almost as much as the food, but Rumford changed all that and laid down the basis of modern methods. As with lighting and heating he first tried out his ideas in the workhouse in Munich, where he completely rebuilt and re-equipped the kitchen and was proud of the fact that he needed to spend only 12 kreutzer (then about 4½d) on fuel to cook a dinner for 1,000 people, which he could certainly not have done with an open fire.

He achieved this by cooking on an embryonic kitchen range, not unlike those used today, together with what came to be called a Rumford roaster. In Rumford's range up to twelve separate fireplaces were built, as vertical holes, into a brickwork structure, and they were designed in shape and size to heat special pots, pans, kettles, double boilers and pressure cookers which Rumford invented. Ovens, roasters and hot water containers could also be built in. The fires could be controlled by opening a register in the ash-pit doors to allow more or less air to flow in, and by using dampers on the individual flues which were all connected to the same chimney. When the range was not in use, earthenware covers could be placed over each separate fireplace and the register almost fully closed, so that the fire could smoulder quietly. The ranges could be made of any size suitable for kitchens of public buildings, such as hospitals, or private houses.

The Rumford roaster was designed for cooking meat which had hitherto been done on a spit over an open fire.

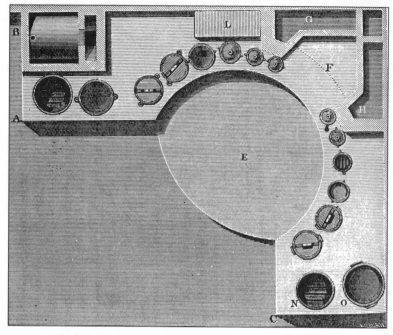

Rumford's design for the kitchen stove in the military hospital in Munich.

The roaster, positioned within the brickwork of a range, consisted of a cylindrical iron container about 60 cm long and 45 cm in diameter. Inside this, the meat was placed on a water-filled dripping-pan to collect the juices, and potatoes and vegetables could be cooked at the same time on a higher shelf. Two 50 mm diameter pipes, each with an adjustable opening, passed below the cylinder and entered it at the rear. They were used to allow more or less air to pass into the cylinder to control the temperature, while a pipe coming out of the top, fitted with a damper, allowed excess gases to escape into a chimney. Rumford claimed that meat roasted in this machine tasted better and was more wholesome than spit-roasted meat. He also found that he could roast 45 kg of veal in six large pieces for a fuel cost of just 3 kreutzers. Not surprisingly the roaster became very popular in many parts of the world. One ironmonger in England fitted 260 over a period of three years and another sold over 200. The minister of the First Church in Salem, Massachusetts, where they still remembered Benjamin Thompson, had one installed in his own home.

Rumford also paid much attention to the general lay-out of the equipment within a kitchen, writing that 'a good arrangement of the different instruments and utensils will tend very much to facilitate the business of cooking, and consequently to put the cook in good humour, which is certainly a matter of serious importance'.[12] He also revolutionized cooking procedures within the army. The old method had involved each individual soldier cooking his own meal in a frying pan resting on a three-legged trivet over an open fire. Rumford invented a portable field stove and, more and more, organized feeding en masse, and this new method was quickly adopted by other European armies.

Alongside his ideas for new equipment and methods, Rumford went to great lengths to provide details of what to cook and how to cook it, producing a veritable cookbook of recipes, particularly of food suitable for the poor using cheap materials such as maize, macaroni, barley and rye. But he picked out the potato, coffee and various soups for special consideration. The potato, which had been introduced into Europe from South America in the middle of the sixteenth century, was not popular among Bavarians. Indeed, many people regarded potatoes as poisonous and believed that they caused consumption and leprosy. However, Thompson demonstrated their virtues so successfully that, within a few years, the potato was the main component of Bavarian diet, and interest in the potato also increased in the rest of Europe. He gave details of how the potatoes should be boiled, depending on their size, to attain the perfection achieved in Lancashire and Ireland, remarking that 'good men will feel that the subject is not unworthy of their attention'.[13] There were specific recipes, too, for the use of potatoes in dumplings and in soups.

As far as drinks were concerned, Rumford, who was very partial to Burton Ale, was a passionate advocate of coffee on which he wrote a special essay, 'Of the Excellent Qualities of Coffee and the Art of Making it in the Highest Perfection'. 'There is more wit in Europe since the use of coffee has become general,'[14] he wrote, and he claimed that sweetened coffee was both wholesome and nourishing, particularly when compared with 'the miserable and unwholesome wash which the poor people in England drink under the name of tea!'[15] He even suggested that coffee could be, for the poor, a satisfactory substitute for alcohol, comparing the 'consciousness of ease, contentment and good will' provided by the former to the 'wild joy and unbridled licentiousness'[16] associated with the latter. And to encourage the use of coffee, he gave details of how it should be stored, brewed and served, even inventing cheap coffee drip-pots for making the drink.

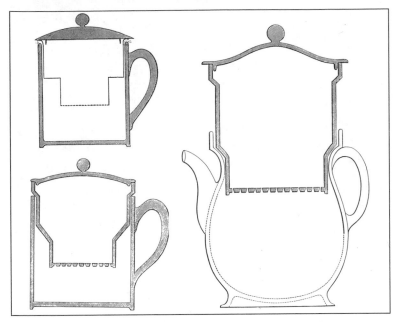

Rumford's original drawings for coffee pots. Top left: a 400 ml cup with a tin strainer; bottom left: an 800 ml cup with a pottery strainer; right: a coffee-pot for making five or six cups.

For feeding the masses, he opted for soups and his best-known concoction came to be called Rumford soup. A simplified recipe read:

Water and peeled barley are put together in a saucepan, and brought to the boil. Peas are then added, and the boiling continued for two hours; then raw, peeled potatoes are added, and the boiling continued for another hour, stirring the contents of the saucepan frequently with a large wooden spoon. Finally, some vinegar, salt, and immediately before serving, pieces of fine wheat bread are added.

There was also brown soup, made by frying rye meal in butter until it was brown, boiling the mix in water, and then adding some seasoning. And a porridge-like mixture, known as samp, which was made by adding maize to a boiled mixture of water, barley meal, pepper, vinegar, herbs and ground red herring. It cost only one-third of a penny for a 500 gram portion, but there were also four up-market recipes costing 1, 2, 4 and 6 pence, with the last one containing some meat. Rumford recommended the addition of small pieces of hard, stale bread to all these soups – the origin of the croûton, perhaps – to encourage proper mastication, writing that in this way 'the enjoyment of eating may be greatly increased and prolonged'.[17]

Rumford's ideas for mass feeding, originally developed in Munich, were adopted all over Europe in the form of soup kitchens. In 1801, for example, upwards of 60,000 poor people in London, out of a population of about a million, were being fed from public kitchens. In Switzerland the meal tickets such kitchens issued were engraved with Rumford's name and portrait. He wrote to Sarah in 1801 that 'it is utterly impossible not to feel deeply affected at these distinguished marks of honour conferred upon me by nations at war with Great Britain, and in countries where I have never been'.[18]

Unfortunately Rumford's researches into the diet of Bavarian soldiers, and the results of some experiments he carried out on the feeding of animals in a veterinary school that he set up in the English Garden, led him to conclude, quite wrongly, that the main nutrient in food was water.

Consequently he watered down all his soups in the firm belief that the new product would be both cheaper and better. However, his views on the nutritive value of water and the resulting thinness of his soups attracted much criticism and he was ridiculed, particularly by William Cobbett (1763–1835), a radical English writer who, like Rumford, was a champion of the poor but also arrogant and quarrelsome. Cobbett regarded it as 'an outrage upon Englishmen that whatever the degree of their poverty, and however nearly they approached starvation, they should have offered to them, in the name of science and charity, the insipid and flatulent compounds which he described as made of dirt and bones'.[19] Other satirists continued in the same vein even after Rumford's death: in 1823 one wrote 'those who can swallow the Count's dinners can swallow anything'.[20]

It seems odd today that someone with Rumford's scientific background and experience could ever have persuaded himself to accept such an erroneous view, but perhaps he can be allowed one error of judgement.

THE ROYAL INSTITUTION

Count Rumford and Sarah arrived in London from Hamburg on 19 September 1798 after a miserable journey. The country through which they travelled was seriously demoralized and crime was rife; the inns were very unpleasant and inhospitable; and on one occasion Sarah had to jump clear of the carriage when the horses came close to tipping it over a precipice. To avoid losses on the exchange of paper notes, a heavy load of coins was being carried so that the party often found it easier to sleep in their carriages. There was one exciting moment for Sarah when Count Taxis caught up with them on the second day of their journey to bid her father a respectful goodbye and to present her with a letter. Alas for her, it was in no way amorous and contained only a few cheerful lines of farewell with no suggestions of regret or sorrow.

Unknown to them, as they were crossing the Channel, a letter was passing in the opposite direction from Lord Grenville, the British Foreign Secretary, to the English Minister in Munich. It read: 'I am to direct you in the last resort to state in distinct terms that His Majesty will by no means consent to receive Count Rumford in the character which has been assigned to him.'[1] King George III and his advisers, who both disliked and distrusted Rumford, had decided that it was quite improper and objectionable for a British subject to reside at the Court of his natural sovereign as a minister of a foreign prince. The fact that the Bavarian government had even suggested this, without any prior consultation, so strained relations between the two countries that they never recovered during Carl Theodore's reign. Rumford had only just arrived at the Royal Hotel when this quite unexpected bad news was passed to him by an official from the Foreign Office. He was granted an audience by the king but nothing came of it, and he became very depressed and began to drink heavily. It was very much out of character, but he did not want to see his friends, even Lady Palmerston. He regarded the whole episode as a massive personal disgrace, and he blamed Carl Theodore's young Electress, rather than the British government, as he slowly realized that his whole political career was probably at an end.

Once again he had to replan his life and, as before, he began to think of returning to America. To that end he wrote to Loammi Baldwin on 28 September 1798 to enquire whether it might be possible to find a 'quiet retreat to which I can retire at some future period and spend the evening of my life'.[2] Sarah, he wrote, was quite 'enchanted with the scheme' and 'I wish to leave her a *home*, something immoveable that she may call her own, as well as the means of subsistence, at my death'.[3] That he should be talking about his death when he was only forty-five is a measure of his despair.

Rumford also made contact with an old friend, the Hon. Rufus King, the American Ambassador in London, to sound him out about the possibilities of a return to America. The situation was somewhat sensitive because Rumford had been proscribed as hostile to the American cause when he first left the country to help the enemy, and the inhabitants of Woburn had voted, in May 1793, 'that the absentees and conspirators, or refugees, ought to be suffered to return, but be excluded from having lot or portion among us'.[4] Rumford's remarkable achievements since leaving were, however, well know across the Atlantic, and there was some support for the view that the slate should be wiped clean and Rumford's past misdeeds conveniently forgotten. As America now faced the possibility of a war with France, both the American Secretary to the Treasury and the Secretary of War thought that Rumford's military expertise would be helpful to upgrade their army. They therefore considered, along with President George Washington, the option of making him either the head of a new American Military Academy or an Inspector General of Artillery. Rumford responded by sending all his military papers, his library and a model of a new portable cannon that he had designed, which was, he said, 'destined as a present to the United States'.[5] He clearly wanted to curry favour and to keep open the chance of continuing his military career.

The Count, deviously as usual, did not tell the Americans that he was also seriously considering alternative plans and they only became aware of them when he wrote to Rufus King on 12 September 1799 that, 'Nothing could have afforded me so much satisfaction as to . . . assist in promoting the prosperity of my native Country . . . but it is not in my power to dissolve those ties by which I am bound.'[6] Those ties, which had been linking together for some time, were to lead to perhaps the greatest of Rumford's achievements: the founding of the Royal Institution of Great Britain.

It cannot have been easy for Rumford to decline the tempting offers he had from America, but when he did so he established himself and Sarah in a house in London. No. 45 Brompton Row (now 168 Brompton Road and occupied by an estate agent's in Knightsbridge) where he said 'the air was good',[7] had five storeys including a basement where the domestic staff lived, and a range of outbuildings including a stable, coach-house and laboratory. Rumford converted it into a veritable showpiece by installing many modern features demonstrating his own particular interests. The house was, as might be expected, very well lit and heated and the outbuildings were connected to it by a centrally heated corridor. All the cooking equipment was individually designed and there was double-glazing in some rooms, together with window-boxes, built-in wardrobes, tables that folded back into the walls, sofa-beds, and drawers beneath the beds for storing sheets and blankets. The finished product was described by Monsieur Pictet as the Elysium, and it made a very suitable and comfortable headquarters from which Rumford could direct his energies in pursuit of his chosen cause.

That cause had grown out of a meeting in England in 1795 between Rumford and Thomas Bernard, the son of Sir Francis Bernard, Governor of Massachusetts from 1760 to 1769. Thomas had been educated at Harvard College and qualified as a lawyer when the family returned to England, but he never practised because he had a speech impediment. After marrying a wealthy heiress, he exerted great influence as what can only be described as a full-time professional philanthropist. He set up the School for the Indigent Blind, the Institution for the Protection and Instruction of Climbing Boys, the Society for the Relief of Poor Neighbours in Distress, the Cancer Institution, the London Fever Hospital, the British Institution for Promoting the Fine Arts in the United Kingdom and the Alfred Club, a literary establishment in which drinking, politics and gambling were banned. He was also the treasurer of the Foundling Hospital where Rumford had reorganized the kitchens.

At their meeting in 1795 Rumford had suggested the setting up in London of workhouses and public kitchens like those he had established in Munich. Consequently he sent Bernard a paper that began by making proposals 'for Forming by Private Subscription, an Establishment for Feeding the Poor and Giving them Useful Employment, and also for furnishing Food at a cheap rate to others who may stand in need of such assistance'.[8] Subsequently Bernard discussed these matters with the anti-slavery campaigner William Wilberforce, Edward James Eliot and the Bishop of Durham in the summer of 1796, and they decided to form a Society for Bettering the Condition of the Poor. The first meeting took place on 21 December 1796, when the king was appointed patron. At the second meeting, on

Benjamin Thompson, Count Rumford.

Rumford's daughter Sarah, aged twenty-one.

The house in which Benjamin Thompson was born.

Woburn, May 6th 1775

Sir, In compliance with your desires I embrace this first opportunity that has offered since I left
Sir. Boston to send you some account of the situation of affairs in this part of the Country—
If you will be so kind as to deliver to
I need not trouble you with a particular account
Doctr .... of Boston, the Papers which I
of the affair at Concord on Wednesday the 19th Ult
left in your care and take his Receipt for the same,
nor of the subsequent gathering at Cambridge &c &c
You will much oblige you have doubtless already
better intelligence of them than I am able to
give you. Your Humble Servant

The only information that I can give you
that can be of any consequence .... they received
Saturday May 6 1775 from a field officer in the Rebel
Army (if that mass of confusion may be called
an Army) & from a member of the Provincial
Congress that is now setting at Watertown. By
them I learn, that an Army consisting of
36,000 effective men is speedily to be raised in
the four New England Governments, & that the
quota for this Province is 13600. That as soon
as this Army shall be raised & regulated it is
generally supposed that the first movement
will be to make a feint attack upon the Town
of Boston, & at the same time to attempt the
Castle with the main body of their Army—
Whether this will be the precise plan of ope-

The first page of Rumford's invisible ink letter. See Appendix I on p. 163. (By permission of the Clements Library, University of Michigan)

Miscellanious Observations upon the state of the
Rebel Army.

Upon Sunday October 15th I saw 16 flat-bottom'd boats
or Batteaus lying just below Cambridge Bridge, & two more
were making in the yard — The workmen informed me
that one was finished every day, and that more workmen
were daily expected from Newbury — These Boats are built
of common deal Boards, & in general will contain from
50 to 60 Men, including the Rowers — What number of them
were to be made I could not learn.

It is generally supposed in the Rebel Army that an
attack is designed upon either Charlestown, or Boston, or
or both — and that these boats are preparing to transport
Troops to those places — But many of the more intelligent
and among these some of their principal Officers, rather
suppose these preparations are only to amuse ye Kings
Troops, and by keeping them continually alarm'd with
apprehension of being attacked, prevent their going to distant parts of the Country to Ravage —

About the 13th October a return was made of the number of Men, that all the boats of every denomination (exclusive of the flat-bottom'd boats,) in the Rebel Camps were
capable of transporting — and I was told by a Person who
saw said return that the total number was 550.

From the best information I have been able to get
with respect to their Military Stores, the total quantity
of Gun Powder that they have in their Camp, (exclusive
of

The first page of the report by Rumford on the state of the rebel army. See Appendix 2 on p. 165. (By permission of the Clements Library, University of Michigan)

Model of Rumford's cannon-boring experiment. (By permission of the Deutsches Museum, München)

ESSAYS,

POLITICAL, ECONOMICAL,

AND

PHILOSOPHICAL.

By BENJAMIN COUNT OF RUMFORD,

KNIGHT OF THE ORDERS OF THE WHITE EAGLE, AND ST. STANISLAUS;
Chamberlain, Privy Counsellor of State, and Lieutenant-General in the Service
of his Most Serene Highness the ELECTOR PALATINE, Reigning DUKE
of BAVARIA ; Colonel of his Regiment of Artillery, and Commander
in Chief of the General Staff of his Army ; F. R. S. Acad. R.
Hiber. Berol. Elec. Boicœ. Palat. et Amer. Soc.

VOL. I.

LONDON:

PRINTED FOR T. CADELL JUN. AND W. DAVIES
(SUCCESSORS TO MR. CADELL) IN THE STRAND.

1796.

The title page of the first edition of Rumford's *Essays*.

The kitchen stove which Rumford built for the kitchen of Baron de Lerchenfeld in Munich.

A Rumford roaster.

Lavoisier and Mme Lavoisier.

Rumford's grave in Auteuil.
(Photograph by Christiane Morin)

Portrait of Rumford aged forty-five.

Medallion of Rumford (1796).

The frontage of the Royal Institution in Albemarle Street (from a drawing by T. Hosmer Shepherd). The columns were added in 1838.

24 February, it was resolved that 'in consideration of the extraordinary services of Count Rumford for the benefit of the poor, and as a testimony of the respect and esteem with which this Society regards his services in the promotion of the general objects of the institution, he be elected and declared a member of the Society and one of the general committee for life'.[9]

The prospects for the Society seemed very bright, helped by a growing feeling among the upper classes that more should be done to aid the poor. The system of having small workhouses within individual parishes had been found wanting, and in 1782 a Bill had been passed in Parliament covering the 'establishment by unions of parishes of reformed workhouses in which the aged, the sick and the infirm, together with their dependent children and all the orphans might be provided for'.[10] In 1795 there was another Bill for 'The Better Relief and Maintenance of the Poor within the Several Hundreds and Districts in England'. And in 1796 William Pitt introduced another for 'The Better Support and Maintenance of the Poor'.

Charity was at last becoming much more acceptable and Rumford wrote to Bernard on 13 May 1798, 'be assured that when you shall have put *doing good* in fashion, you will have done all that human wisdom can do to retard and prolong the decline of a great and powerful nation that has arrived at, or passed, the zenith of human glory'.[11] He also wrote that 'we must make benevolence fashionable'[12] and that, so far as he himself was concerned, he was 'actuated merely and simply by a desire to do good, and promote the happiness and prosperity of society'.[13]

It might then have been assumed that Rumford was almost in the 'cometh the hour, cometh the man' mould and that he and Bernard must make a very powerful team. They were indeed both men of strong character, and perhaps because of this they did not always see eye to eye. Their first dispute arose because Rumford's original paper sent to Bernard had contained *two* proposals. The first was well reflected in the general aims of the Society for Bettering the Conditions of the Poor, but Rumford's second proposal was that there should be a 'connected institution for Introducing and bringing forward into general Use, new Inventions and Improvements, particularly such as relate to the Management of Heat and the Saving of Fuel'.[14] He wanted to apply science to improve living standards because he thought that 'the vivifying rays of science, when properly directed, tend to excite the activity and increase the energy of an enlightened nation'.[15] But Bernard and some of the other Society members thought that Rumford's ideas were far too ambitious and were not keen to adopt them. A committee of eight members was set up to examine the issue and, at an important meeting on 31 January 1799, Rumford was asked to modify his proposals. He responded by proposing, in a fifty-page pamphlet, the 'formation by Subscription, in the Metropolis of the British Empire, of a Public Institution for diffusing the Knowledge and facilitating the general Introduction of useful Mechanical Inventions and Improvements, and for teaching by courses of Philosophical Lectures and Experiments, the Application of Science to the Common Purposes of Life'.[16] This eventually became the Royal Institution of Great Britain.

The idea was extremely well received and subscriptions rolled in. Original founders and sole proprietors had to pay 50 guineas, life members 10 guineas, and annual members 2 guineas each year. Within a short time £5,000 had been promised and the first meeting of the proprietors, many of them already famous, was held at the home of Sir Joseph Banks at 32 Soho Square in London. The venue was well chosen because Banks, an intimate friend of Rumford's, had already been the President of the Royal Society since 1778 and it was important that the proposed new Institution should complement its work and not compete with it. Banks, moreover, was an experienced scientist and administrator. Born in 1744, he had been educated at Harrow, Eton and Oxford, and was well known internationally as an explorer and botanist. He had travelled in Newfoundland between 1766 and 1768, collecting plants; he had equipped James Cook's ship *Endeavour* at his own expense and sailed in it on its voyage round the world between 1768 and 1771; and he had visited the Hebrides and Iceland in 1772. In addition, he had suggested the colonization of New South Wales in Australia by transported criminals, and he was both wealthy and a friend of the king.

Banks chaired the meeting, at which nine managers were appointed to run the new organization with Rumford, Banks and Bernard playing the leading roles. A month later it was decided to buy a property in Albemarle Street at a cost of £4,500; it still houses the Institution today. An architect, Mr Thomas Webster, who also ran a successful school for training mechanics, was appointed and work began on converting what had been a large private house. The enormous ballroom became a lecture theatre; the servants' quarters in the basement were replaced by a kitchen fitted with a Rumford range and Rumford roasters, and by laboratories; and all the rooms were equipped with Rumford stoves. Space was also planned for two of Rumford's pet projects: a school for mechanics, where Mr Webster would teach a group of twenty working-class young men, who would live in the attic of the Institution, over a 3–4 month period, and a Repository of rooms containing models of 'that most curious and most useful machine, the steam engine'[17] and 'models of all such other machines and useful instruments as the managers shall deem worthy of public notice'.[18]

Rumford wanted the new organisation to be a reliable source of information and also of teaching about 'new applications of science to the useful purposes of life'.[19] To provide the teaching, Dr Thomas Garnett, a successful Professor of Natural Philosophy at the Anderson's Institution in Glasgow, an organization not unlike the Royal Institution, was appointed as Professor and Public Lecturer in Experimental Philosophy, Mechanics and Chemistry. He was a practising doctor, who had built up a fine reputation as a popular lecturer. On the condition that he brought all his own lecture equipment with him, he was offered accommodation in the Institution, with a salary of £300 per year; a long list of possible lecture subjects was drawn up by Rumford; and he was to start work at the end of 1799.

Before then, in August, Sarah had decided to return to America. She had lived with her father in Brompton Road for a year since they arrived from Munich but she was less keen to stay in England than he was. Moreover, her relationship with her father had deteriorated since the collapse of her affair with Count Taxis and her discovery that she had an illegitimate half-sister. Nor did she have many friends in England, though Lady Palmerston was always extremely good to her. She also had a mild affair with one of her father's best friends Sir Charles Blagden, a distinguished physician and the secretary or the Royal Society, but nothing came of it. So she wrote that 'she could breathe only the air of America'[20] and sailed for home on 25 August 1799.

Rumford did not refer to her departure much and in some ways life would probably have been easier for him without her had it not been for the fact that he was taken ill soon after she left. His health had never been good and he had been off work a number of times over the years, probably because of stomach ulcers that caused him to adopt peculiar eating habits and to drink nothing but water. On this occasion he recuperated by spending much of the time with Lady Palmerston at her country house at Broadlands and travelling around Britain, but it took him almost four months to recover.

While he was ill, Rumford had written to Pictet to say, confidentially, that he was 'far from sanguine as to the success of our undertaking'[21] and, as the nineteenth century began, he redoubled his efforts to bring his brainchild to fruition. In particular he left Brompton Road to go to live at the Institution in Albemarle Street so that he could take more direct control and he issued a new prospectus which he distributed very widely, sending copies, for example, to the heads of every American college. The prospectus[22] appealed specially to the wealthy, and epitomized Rumford's hopes and ideals in the paragraph: 'When the rich shall take pleasure in contemplating and encouraging such mechanical improvements as are really useful, good taste, with its inseparable companion, good morals, will revive; rational economy will become fashionable; industry and ingenuity will be honoured and rewarded; and the pursuits of all the various classes of society will then tend to promote the public prosperity.'

The Royal Seal was granted in January 1800, and the Royal Institution of Great Britain held its first official meeting on 11 March. This gave the outward impression that all was going well but a quarrelsome atmosphere was already building up behind the scenes, not helped by Rumford's dictatorial presence. If he couldn't actually do it himself he wanted everything, right down to the last detail, done his way. The political commentator Peter Pindar wrote: 'Although a man may, like the Count, possess *extraordinary intellect*, and though a man may be the *best judge of himself*, nevertheless it is *indecorous* to treat the opinions of *others* with contempt.'[23] The arguments were about personnel, organization and money, and if Rumford was on one side Bernard was generally on the other. In the prevailing atmosphere, almost everybody was involved in some quarrel or dispute.

The porter and his wife, the housekeeper, were sacked because it was claimed they were sullen and impudent. Thomas Webster found that his plans for the design of a temporary lecture hall, drawn up on Rumford's instructions, were rubbished by some of the other governors who passed them to another architect for revision and it was only Rumford's intervention which saved the day for him.

Garnett, too, was unhappy. He began his lectures immediately after the official opening of the Institution on

A cartoon by James Gillray of a lecture at the Royal Institution about 1801. Professor Garnett is administering nitrous oxide to the gentleman on the left. Humphry Davy, who discovered the anaesthetic properties of the gas, is holding the bellows, and Count Rumford is standing by the door on the right.

4 March even though building work was going on all around. There were two series of lectures, one for the general public who wanted to be entertained and another for those who wanted a university-type course in science. They each took place, one at 2 p.m. and the other at 8 p.m., three times a week for three months. The lectures were very well received but Garnett felt hard done by. His wife had died on Christmas Day 1798, leaving him with two young daughters, but there was no room for them in his apartment at the Royal Institution so they had to stay with relatives. He also found that he was not allowed to supplement his income by practising as a doctor as he had done in Glasgow.

Rumford himself also had to face severe setbacks. His idea that Webster should teach a group of mechanics was dropped because Bernard, Banks and other managers were against it. An early opportunity of improving technical education in the country was therefore lost, and something of an argument developed as to whether the Institution should serve the wealthy gentry, who could provide the necessary funds, or the poor mechanics and artisans who needed help. It was an early 'them and us' dilemma, with the wealthy Banks claiming that artisans had their place in society and that to educate them was 'to force them like hot-bed plants out of the sphere in which they are so useful'.[24]

Rumford's idea for a shop window for new inventions was also strongly opposed by Bernard and turned down because it was thought it would be far too expensive.

Moreover, the idea was anathema to manufacturers, such as Boulton and Watt, the successful makers of steam engines. They feared that all their closely guarded trade secrets would be on display, allowing competitors to copy their ideas and breach their patents. To emphasize the point Matthew Boulton refused a request to become a manager.

It was a measure, then, of his eternal optimism that Rumford could write to Professor Pictet on 5 July that 'my exertions have been completely successful – my competitors have been defeated and all my plans have been adopted without any alterations'.[25] This is even more remarkable because his exertions had in fact made him ill again and he was off work for almost five months, first taking the waters in Harrogate, a well-known spa in Yorkshire, for two months, and then travelling in Scotland.

When Rumford returned to the Royal Institution late in 1800, some thorny problems were still unresolved. The foremost concerned the position of Professor Garnett and it soon became clear that Rumford wanted to get rid of him. His 1800 lectures had been very successful and he was now preparing for his new series in the newly completed lecture theatre. But he made the mistake of publishing the details without any consultation with the managers and this so infuriated Rumford that he set up a committee to oversee the use of Garnett's time and to vet the contents of his lectures. Poor Garnett also found that, despite earlier promises, his pay was frozen, and on 9 February he learnt, out of the blue, that Humphry Davy had been appointed as his assistant, and that he was expected to give up one of his

Sir Humphry Davy.

rooms to the newcomer. It was all too much and, broken in spirit, he resigned on 1 June. He turned to medicine again and practised in London, but within a year he caught typhus from one of his patients and died, leaving his young daughters destitute.

Apart from the unfortunate effect it had on Garnett's situation, the appointment of Davy was a master stroke and may well have been the most important thing that Rumford ever did. Born in Penzance in 1778, Davy was the son of a wood carver, and at the age of seventeen he was apprenticed to a local surgeon. After two years he turned his attention to chemistry and went to work for Thomas Beddoes at the Medical Pneumatic Institution in Bristol. Beddoes believed that lung diseases could be cured by the inhalation of mixtures of different gases, and Davy, working in this field, rapidly built up a good reputation by doing many of his experiments on himself. In this way he discovered the physiological effect of nitrous oxide, nicknamed laughing gas because it made some people feel hilarious when they breathed it, but nearly killed himself by inhaling carbon monoxide, the poisonous component of coal gas.

Davy's work was brought to Rumford's notice by Mr R.J. Underwood, a proprietor of the Royal Institution, and, after being interviewed by a committee consisting of

Rumford, Banks and Henry Cavendish, he was offered his new job. He was only twenty-three years old, but he was appointed Assistant Lecturer in Chemistry, Director of the Chemical Laboratory and Assistant Editor of the Journals of the Institution. His salary was 100 guineas per annum, he was given one of Garnett's rooms to live in and he was provided with coals and candles.

It was a lucky break for everyone. There was some doubt initially as to how his Cornish accent, his scruffy appearance and his general cockiness would go down in fashionable circles in London but it all turned out unexpectedly well, perhaps because, then as now, the general public like their scientists to be a bit eccentric. Not only did he become an internationally famous scientist, he also proved to be a very popular lecturer, so much so, that attending his lectures became the thing to do for upper-class Londoners. Albemarle Street was so blocked with elegant carriages that a one-way system had to be introduced, and nothing like it had ever been seen before. J.A. Paris, Davy's biographer, records that 'men of the first rank and talent, – the literary and the scientific, the practical and the theoretical, blue-stockings, and women of fashion, the old and the young, all crowded – eagerly crowded – the lecture-room. His youth, his simplicity, his natural eloquence, his chemical knowledge, his happy illustrations and well-conducted experiments, excited universal attention and unbounded applause'.[26] It was no surprise, then, that after just one year his salary was doubled because he had 'given the most satisfactory proofs of his ability as a lecturer and of his indefatigable zeal'.[27]

This upturn in the fortunes of the Royal Institution was greatly helped when Thomas Young was appointed as Professor Garnett's successor in July 1801. He was born in Milverton in Somerset in 1773 and after studying medicine in London, Edinburgh, Göttingen and Cambridge, he practised in London before turning to research. He is best remembered as the originator of the undulatory theory of light and for his work in deciphering the inscriptions on the Rosetta stone, unearthed in Egypt in 1799. Though mainly self-taught, he had a prodigious talent. It is claimed that he read the whole Bible twice when he was two; by thirteen he was proficient in eight languages, including Hebrew, Chaldean, Syriac and Sumerian; at sixteen he translated Shakespeare into Greek iambics; he was known as 'Phenomenon Young' at Cambridge; and at the age of just twenty-one he was elected as a member of the Royal Society. The connection of such a scholar with the Royal Institution greatly enhanced its prestige, but he was not a good lecturer and he stayed for only two years. Thereafter he worked as a doctor at St George's Hospital in London until he died in 1829.

One of the side-effects of Young's arrival in Albemarle Street was that Rumford moved out to make way for him, and returned to his house in Brompton Row. This took him away from the day-to-day management of the Institution, which was handed over to Young, and as the organization seemed to be running well Rumford's thoughts turned inwards and he became anxious again about his finances and his future. He was still in receipt of half-pay as a retired

British colonel but he was unsure about the continuance of his pension from Bavaria, and thought that he ought to visit that country again to renew his contacts and to see whether he might be able to organize a summer residence there. He did not want to be away for long lest he lose touch with the Royal Institution, but he set off for Munich in September, completing the journey in only ten days.

The situation in Bavaria had changed considerably. Carl Theodore had died after suffering a stroke in February 1799 and had been replaced by Maximilian Joseph, the former Duke of Deux-Ponts. One of the first actions of the new Elector had been to strip Rumford of his military command in Bavaria, though he had not removed his pension. In addition, the alliance between Theodore and George III seemed to be slipping because Maximilian had served as an officer in the French Army and Britain was now at war with that country. So Rumford was very relieved when he found that his welcome was wholeheartedly friendly. He only stayed for ten days but everything was arranged as he had wanted. He saw Sophy Baumgarten and found her clever and charming, he went to visit the Princess of Taxis in Dischingen and stayed with one of his favourite mistresses, Laura de Kalb, writing that 'it is impossible not to love her with the most tender affection'.[28] The Elector even invited him to return to preside over an academy of arts and sciences that was to be set up in Munich.

Rumford's reception in France, on his way back to England, was even warmer. Although the two countries were at war and Rumford was still a colonel in the British

Army, he described his reception, on his first visit to Paris, as 'simply enchantment'. Everyone seemed to know his name and to be familiar with his inventions; he met Napoleon, the First Consul, Talleyrand, the Foreign Minister, and scientists such as Volta, Lagrange, Laplace, Berthollet and Fourcroy; and he was elected to the *Institut National de France* which had replaced the older *Académie des Sciences* in 1793. He was only a second class member, reflecting his achievements as a politician rather than as a scientist, but it was nevertheless a singular honour because there were only twenty-four foreign members, and he was elected alongside Thomas Jefferson, the President of the United States.

That was a real feather in his cap, but he probably enjoyed meeting the ladies even more. On 13 November he met Madame Laplace and 'on coming away made many excuses for having kept her in bed till so late an hour';[29] on 20 November he found Madame Jollien with 'her bosom moderately uncovered . . . and with eyes by far the most beautiful I had ever beheld';[30] and on 8 December Madame de Staël assured him that she was a 'most loving mistress'.[31] But it was Mme Lavoisier, the widow of the famous French chemist Antoine Lavoisier, whom he first met on 19 November, who in the end made the greatest impact on him and six years later he married her.

All these activities meant that Rumford stayed in France much longer than had been planned and it is not surprising that he was reluctant to leave when he compared his life in Munich and Paris with that to which he had become accustomed in London. When he did return, on 20 December, he found that his situation had worsened. Cadell and Davies did not want to publish any more of his writings because the public had lost interest in them, his opponents had increased their influence in the Royal Institution, and even Lady Palmerston, perhaps having heard of his antics in Paris, was not ready with her usual welcome.

Feeling that he was no longer wanted in London, he decided at the start of 1802 that he would go back across the Channel where the grass seemed distinctly greener. Accordingly, he started to tidy up his affairs. He completed a collection of *Philosophical Papers* on which he had been working for some time, and persuaded his publishers to print them; the work was dedicated to His Most Serene Highness Maximilian Joseph, Elector Palatine of Bavaria. He wrote an outlandishly optimistic progress report on the Royal Institution, in which he claimed that it could be considered as 'finished and firmly established'. And, after drawing up a 35-page inventory of his house in Brompton Road, which even itemized a rat trap, he left England, never to return, on 9 May 1802.

His departure left a number of loose ends and, because Banks was suffering from gout, it fell to Bernard and a small committee to pick up the pieces. The major problem that confronted them was the desperate state of the Institute's finances, caused by the fall in subscriptions from £11,047 in 1800 to £3,474 in 1801 and £2,999 in 1802. Rumford's final report had claimed a balance of £8,100, but in fact there was only £3,180 in the bank and outstanding debts of £3,474. So at the start of 1803 serious consideration was given to closing the Institution and selling its property to pay off its debts. Fortunately this was avoided by pursuing a strict policy of cost-cutting and retrenchment. An external accountant was called in and, among other things, contracting out some of the services was examined, the amount of literature being distributed was greatly reduced, and many of the staff were made redundant. Thomas Webster, for example, who had been there from the beginning, was paid off with £50; he later became secretary of the Geological Society and curator of its museum, and a Professor of Geology at London University before dying in 1844. More importantly, it was finally realized that Rumford's original ideas had been too ambitious and it was decided to concentrate the activities around the lectures and the laboratories.

These were where Davy's strengths lay and it was he who led the Institution forward. His lectures continued to be regarded as major social and scientific events, and his successes as a researcher, particularly the isolation of the elements potassium, sodium, barium, calcium, strontium and magnesium in 1807 and 1808 brought international renown both to him and to the institution. There was, however, another financial crisis in 1809, when it was found that both the capital and the annual income were insufficient to support the operation adequately. The Institution was still a private body, owned and run by the proprietors, but this was changed by an Act of Parliament in

1810. The proprietors were compensated or made life members, and a new governing body was elected by all the members. The Institution therefore became more of a government body and its laboratory was made available for general use, but it remained the most elegant social and philosophic club in London and continued to thrive.

Davy was knighted in 1812 and, when he married the rich widow Mrs Apreece three days later he was able to resign his professorship, though he was appointed an honorary professor a year later, and he continued to work in the Institution. He invented the miner's safety lamp in 1815, and he succeeded Joseph Banks as President of the Royal Society in 1820 before being taken ill in 1827 and dying two years later in 1829.

In 1833 Michael Faraday, the third son of an ailing blacksmith, whom Davy had employed as a laboratory assistant in 1813, was himself appointed Professor of Chemistry at the Royal Institution and he was an even greater success than Davy. In 1818 he made the first high-quality alloys; in 1823 he liquefied chlorine and other gases; in 1825 he isolated benzene; in 1826 he began the annual Christmas lectures which are still held to this day and now transmitted live on national television; and in 1835 he put forward the basic laws of electrolysis. In addition, over the years he discovered, along with Joseph Henry in America, the phenomenon of electromagnetic induction, and also contributed to the invention of the dynamo and the electric motor.

Probably the world's greatest experimental physicist and described by one contemporary as being able to 'smell the truth', Faraday spent forty-nine years at the Royal Institution until 1862. Since then there have been many other research directors including nine Nobel Prize winners and such famous men as John Tyndall, James Dewar, William Bragg, Lawrence Bragg and George Porter. For the first time a female director, Professor Susan Greenfield, was appointed in 1998. It is interesting to reflect on what Rumford might have thought of that, but, were he here today, he could be justly proud of what, despite much difficulty and some personal cost, he founded.

A FEMALE DRAGON

Rumford's decision to leave England and the Royal Institution was probably influenced by an earlier agreement he had made in Munich that he would spend six months of every year in Bavaria in return for the maintenance of his pension. On 9 May 1802 he set out once more on the journey from London to Munich, which he had first taken nineteen years earlier. He stopped off in Paris to see Mme Lavoisier and stayed rather longer than he had planned, at Maximilian's request, to try to influence French opinion in favour of extending the Bavarian border near Liechtenstein. But he found that his influence in France had greatly waned since his last triumphant visit because Anglo-French relationships had deteriorated. Napoleon never spoke to him and his freedom of movement was hampered by bureaucracy because he was English. So, reluctantly leaving behind Mme Lavoisier, he set off for Munich on 10 August 1802, accompanied by his old friend Sir Charles Blagden.

His reception in Bavaria was warm enough but, as in France, he was not the power in the land that he had once been, and when Blagden left at the beginning of October there was little or nothing for him to do. He would have liked to return to Mme Lavoisier but he had agreed to stay in Bavaria for six months. Moreover, relations between France and England were still unhappy so that a return to France was not possible immediately. Rumford, therefore established himself in a large house, turned his attention to his favourite scientific subject – heat – and collected enough material together to produce papers in 1804 on 'An Inquiry concerning the Nature of Heat, and the Mode of its Communication'[1] and 'Reflections on Heat'.[2]

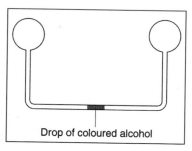

Drop of coloured alcohol

Rumford's thermoscope.

The positive outcome of this work was the invention of a number of thermometers, with different shapes and of different sizes, and of what Rumford called a thermo-scope. This consisted of two small globes, each 40 mm in diameter, containing air, which were connected by a horizontal tube in which there was a drop of coloured alcohol. When the two globes were at the same temperature, the alcohol drop was in the centre of the tube, but it moved along the tube when one globe was heated or cooled. The thermoscope did not measure temperature but was a very sensitive detector of temperature differences.

Rumford used these thermometers to experiment on the nature of heat transmission by radiation. In one series of experiments he filled a hollow brass cylinder with water, in which a thermometer was immersed. The water started at 50°F above room temperature and Rumford measured the time it took for the temperature to drop by 10°F. He then covered the cylinder with different materials of various colours and textures, and compared the resulting cooling times. In one experiment he used two cylinders covered with gold-beater's skin (an animal membrane used to separate leaves of gold during beating), one painted black to represent a negro, and the other white to represent a white man. He found that 'the negro cooled considerably more rapidly than the white man, requiring 23½ minutes to cool through 10 degrees, while the white man required 28 minutes'.[3]

In a second series of experiments he used his thermoscope to compare the heat radiated by two different cylinders. To do this he allowed the heat from one cylinder to fall on to the left-hand globe of the thermoscope, and the heat from the other to fall on to the right-hand globe. By moving the cylinders closer to or further from the globes he could find the point at which they radiated equally, and this enabled him to compare the two radiations. He concluded that the shinier a surface the more slowly it cooled, and that a dull surface cooled more quickly. In other words, shiny surfaces radiate heat less quickly than dull ones. This, he pointed out, meant that polished tea pots and pans kept their contents hot longer than dull ones, and explained why the negro cooled considerably more rapidly than the white man. He also applied the principle in his everyday life by wearing white clothes and a shiny white hat in winter – which soon gained him a reputation as an eccentric.

His work certainly advanced his understanding of heat, yet on some points he was still muddled, which at least proves that he was not omnipotent. Although he had recognized that heat was motion and had discarded the caloric theory, he did not regard cold as an absence of heat, but rather as something different from heat. He spoke, for example, of a hot body emitting calorific rays while a cold body emitted frigorific rays. Because he also likened these rays to light rays he supported the view that all space was occupied by a hypothetical medium called the aether or ether. This was an old but well-established Greek idea which had been used by William Gilbert in his theories of electricity and magnetism and by William Harvey to explain how the sun's heat kept animals warm. More recently, in 1678 the Dutch astronomer Christiaan Huygens had resurrected it as part of his wave theory of light because he thought it was necessary for there to be some medium through which light waves could pass, and Rumford thought likewise regarding his calorific or frigorific rays. But with the acceptance of Albert Einstein's theory of relativity at the start of the twentieth century, the idea of an all-permeating ether was no longer necessary.

Rumford had been preoccupied but rather lonely during the winter and spring months in Munich and had been hoping to be able to return to France. However, the insecure peace between England and France that followed the signing of the Treaty of Amiens in March 1802 soon broke down and war was declared again on 18 May 1803. So he was pleased when he heard from Mme Lavoisier in June that she had obtained permission to travel to Munich, and for them to have a holiday together in Switzerland.

He was fifty years old and had been a widower for eleven years; she was forty-three and a widow for nine. Born Marie-Anne-Pierrette Paulze, the daughter of a receiver and farmer-general of taxes, she was brought up in a cultured and civilized household frequented by many well-known philosophers. She married the brilliant Antoine Laurent Lavoisier, sometimes referred to as the 'father of modern chemistry', when she was only thirteen and he was twenty-eight and she grew up to be a clever, strong-willed woman with a striking beauty, a radiant personality and great social charm. She was renowned as an exciting French hostess whose parties attracted scientists from all over the world. During her twenty-two years of married life with Lavoisier she acted as a research and library assistant to him and helped with the writing and illustration of his papers. As she was also a very good linguist she translated foreign papers, such as those of Joseph Priestley and Henry Cavendish, for him.

Unfortunately in 1768 Lavoisier had become a farmer-general of taxes, like his father-in-law, to provide more money for his researches and this led to him being charged, in 1794, with involvement in a conspiracy 'against the French people tending to favour by all possible means the success of the enemies of France'.[4] One of the alleged crimes was 'adding to tobacco, water and other ingredients detrimental to the health of the citizens'.[5] He was found guilty, along with his father-in-law and twenty-six others, by a revolutionary tribunal and they were all beheaded on 8 May 1794 in the Place de la Révolution (now the Place de la Concorde). Lavoisier mounted the guillotine as number 4, after his father-in-law, who was number 3.

There can have been few more blatantly political and senseless murders than that of Lavoisier. A Liberal, he recognized the need for change in France but opposed revolutionary methods. He gave a lifetime of service to his country as a scientist, a tax reformer, a *régisseur des poudres* who transformed the French gunpowder industry, an agricultural reformer, and a member of the provincial assembly of Orléans. Yet the tribunal's vice-president said that 'the Republic has no need of men of science',[6] a view countered by Joseph Lagrange, a contemporary French mathematician, who wrote: 'It required but a moment to strike off this head, and probably another hundred years will not suffice to reproduce such another'.[7]

The sudden loss of both husband and father in one day was a tragedy for Mme Lavoisier and for some time she had to live with the real possibility that she would face a similar fate. She had, moreover, made many enemies who claimed that she could have done more to save her husband's life if she had been less accusatory and more pleading to those who brought him to his death. She wisely left Paris for a few months and a year later, when many of the revolutionaries had lost their own heads, she was able to re-establish her old position as a formidable hostess and once again attracted many scientists to her salon. And this is how Rumford first met her on 19 November 1801.

Romance was obviously in the air. After his third meeting with her, Rumford wrote in his journal on 2 December that

'Mme Lavoisier is a very friendly, cheerful good-natured woman and she is rich and independent. Speaking of my philosophical pursuits and intended publications I observed that nothing amused me so much as making experiments but that it was tiresome to write an account of them. She said to me "Venez vous établier ici et je veux être votre secrétaire, vous travaillerez et moi j'écrirai". "That would be charming indeed" was my answer.'[8]

As Mme Lavoisier was also fond of travel it is not surprising that their holiday in Switzerland was very successful even though it was for Rumford at least, a mixture of business with pleasure. He took with him quite a lot of equipment and papers, and while in Geneva lectured to scientists on his recent work. And when they stayed with Professor Pictet in a chalet close to Chamonix, he spent time investigating some rather mysterious pits, about 18 cm in diameter and up to 1.5 metres deep, and full of water, in the surface of the ice on the Mer de Glace. He learnt that such pits occur only during the hot summer months, and he realized that this extraordinary phenomenon was probably related to some earlier work that he and others had done which showed that water had a maximum density at approximately 41°F. His explanation was that the water on the surface of a small pot-hole, heated by a warming wind to a temperature between 32 and 41°F, would have a higher density than the cooler water below it. It would therefore sink to the bottom of the hole, melt some of the ice there and so deepen the hole.

At the end of their travels, Mme Lavoisier returned to France determined to persuade the authorities to allow

Rumford into the country. He stayed in Mannheim, close to the border, to await her call, and he was eventually granted permission to live in Paris, at 356 rue de Clichy.

Sarah had not been told by her father of his activities, though Blagden, who had himself once flirted with Mme Lavoisier, had kept her informed to some extent. However, she did hear directly from her father when he wrote on 22 January 1804: 'I shall withhold this information from you no longer. I really do think of marrying, though I am not yet absolutely determined on matrimony. I made the acquaintance of this very amiable woman in Paris, who, I believe, would have no objection to having me for a husband, and who in all respects would be a proper match for me. She is a widow, without children, never having had any; is about my own age, enjoys good health, is very pleasant in society, has a handsome fortune at her own disposal, enjoys a most respectable reputation, keeps a good house, which is frequented by all the first Philosophers and men of eminence in the science and literature of the age, or rather of Paris. And what is more than all the rest, is goodness itself. . . . She has been very handsome in her day, and even now, at 46 or 48, is not bad-looking; of a middling size, but rather *en bon point* than thin. She has a great deal of vivacity, and writes incomparably well.'[9] And he wrote to Lady Palmerston on 8 February to tell her he expected to be married by May.

In the event, such an early date turned out to be over-optimistic and the marriage finally took place about eighteen months later. The unexpected delay was caused by the unforeseen legal requirement for Rumford to produce his birth certificate and his wife's death certificate – she had died in January 1792 – from America. He therefore wrote to Sarah on 2 July to ask if she would obtain these documents, but because of the state of the war between France and England there were only very few ships sailing across the Atlantic so the papers did not arrive in Paris until the end of 1804, and they still had to run the gauntlet of French bureaucracy.

Meanwhile he spent much of his time on scientific pursuits and on the activities of the *Institut National de France*. Originally elected to that élite society in 1801, his membership was upgraded in 1803 to First Class in recognition of his scientific achievements. He was one of only seven foreign First Class members, which greatly enhanced his reputation and he took the opportunity of presenting many papers giving his latest views on topics associated with heat and light. His membership also brought him into close contact with France's foremost scientists, and he participated in their discussions in which Napoleon, who was also a First Class member, frequently took part.

In June 1805 Rumford was called back to Munich by the Elector, to consider setting up the proposed new Academy of Arts and Sciences. Once again he received a friendly welcome, including an addition of 4,000 florins to his annual pension, as a premature wedding present, but events soon took a turn for the worse. The Austrian emperor, tired of trying to persuade Bavaria to enter a German coalition, invaded the country and seemed likely to launch an attack on Munich. At this, Maximilian and his court fled to Mannheim and Rumford quickly wound up his affairs. He returned to Paris along with six members of the Aichner family who had been his faithful servants ever since he first set foot in Munich and who he thought might be in danger from an advancing Austrian army.

It was the middle of September when he arrived back in Paris, where he found that the paperwork necessary for his wedding was all in order. Satisfactory financial arrangements had been agreed and the couple had bought a grand house in the Rue d'Anjou close to the Tuileries Gardens and the Champs-Elysées. It had cost 6,000 guineas and was set in a beautiful 2 acre garden; it was approached through an iron gate alongside a porter's lodge, via a winding avenue. Rumford referred to it as 'this paradise of a place, made what it is by me – my money, skill and directions'.[10]

Everything then was in place, and the wedding ceremony took place in the Town Hall on 24 October. The event was recorded, somewhat scathingly, in the *Literary Tablet* in London:

> Married; in Paris, Count Rumford to the widow of Lavoisier; by which nuptial experiment he obtains a fortune of 8,000 pounds per annum – the most effective of all the Rumfordizing projects for keeping a house warm.

Perhaps it was a bad omen that Madame wanted to retain a link with her famous past by insisting that she be known as Countess Lavoisier de Rumford.

The next day, however, Rumford seemed to be very happy and he wrote to Sarah saying that he 'had the best-founded hopes of passing my days in peace and quiet in this paradise of a place'.[11] His hopes, alas, were soon dashed because, although the married couple had known each other for almost five years, they soon discovered that they were incompatible and began to argue about almost everything. The countess liked entertainment and small talk, but he preferred quiet contemplation and experiment. She liked good food and wine, but his stomach couldn't take it, so he commonly sat at a separate table when they had guests. She and her own servants disliked the Aichner family, except for one of the girls, so Rumford had to send them back to Munich. He loved music, but she didn't care for it. And she objected to the way in which he kept altering the house and its contents to suit his own tastes without any reference to hers.

It was a case of two strong-willed people, accustomed to doing things their own way, who could not – or would not – adapt. Rumford wrote to Sarah, two months after his marriage, 'Between you and myself, as a family secret, I am not at all sure that two certain persons were not wholly mistaken, in their marriage, as to each other's characters. Time will tell.'[12] But time recorded nothing but deterioration, and on the first anniversary of his wedding Rumford wrote again to Sarah. 'Very likely she is as much disaffected towards me as I am towards her. Little it matters with me, but I call her a female Dragon.'[13]

A year later, on the second anniversary, he wrote: 'I am still here, and so far from things getting better they get worse every day. We are more violent and more open . . . in our quarrels.'[14] And with obvious reluctance he recounted one such quarrel. The countess had invited a large party to the house, but Rumford did not like her choice of guests and thought she had picked them just to vex him. He therefore walked down the drive to the lodge, locked the iron gates, took the keys away, and told the porter not to let anyone in. When the guests arrived, the embarrassed countess could do nothing other than try to explain the situation to them over a high brick wall. Afterwards, to get her own back, she poured boiling water over some of his most precious flowers in the garden.

Things went from bad to worse. Rumford wrote to Sarah on 12 April 1808, describing his wife as 'the most imperious, tyrannical unfeeling woman that ever existed, and whose perseverance in pursuing an object is equal to her profound cunning and wickedness in framing it.'[15] He said that he could not call her a lady, that it was impossible to continue, and spoke of separation and of buying a small, handsome house that he had seen in Auteuil about 6 kilometres from the centre of Paris.

The separation did not, however, materialize for over a year because of difficulties over financial matters. The countess had contributed most to the cost of their house and had deposited 120,000 livres in 5 per cent French bonds in the bank, in Rumford's name, to be left to Sarah in the event of their deaths. On the other hand, Rumford had spent a lot of his own money on renovations and alterations to the house. Neither party was prepared to give ground,

Rumford referring to his wife's 'implacable hatred and malice',[16] and it required arbitration by friends to resolve the issues. It was not then until 30 June 1809 that the divorce papers were signed, and for the previous three months Rumford had been very ill in bed.

Now that he was free he wrote: 'I find myself relieved from an almost impossible burden . . . and am gaining every day in health. . . . Oh! happy, thrice happy, am I, to be my own man again.'[17] So the tortuous path of Rumford's life took its final twist and he moved to the house he had bought, rather expensively, in April 1808. No. 59 rue d'Auteuil was to be his last home. It was perhaps not a happy omen that the previous owner was a party-giving friend of his ex-wife, but the house had a 3-acre garden and was well situated between the Seine and the Bois de Boulogne. It seemed an ideal place for Rumford to savour the 'sweets of quiet, liberty and independence'[18] in retirement and philosophical pursuits.

He was, however, at a low ebb and had few friends to whom he could turn. He had fallen out with one of his oldest allies, Sir Charles Blagden, and many of his other English contemporaries viewed with some displeasure his life in a hostile country which was threatening from time to time to invade England. Nor had he made many new friends in France. Indeed, as in Munich he had made some enemies because some of the scientists, notably the Marquis de Laplace, a somewhat despotic leader of the *Institut*, did not take kindly to his strongly expressed views on what he thought were the errors of their thinking. Rumford thought, too, that his wife used her influence to undermine him. Nor had their very public squabbling caused anything other than ridicule and laughter in Parisian society.

Fortunately he still had support from his old allies in Bavaria. Maximilian, who was crowned King of Bavaria on 1 January 1806 as a reward for supporting Napoleon in the harsh campaign against Austria and Russia, wrote to him, and 'encouraged him to bear his misfortunes like a man of firmness who had nothing to reproach himself with'.[19] But his main hopes for the future rested on Sarah. He had kept her fully informed about the gruesome details of his marriage, and had asked her more than once to come to Paris. Now he tried even more persuasively, writing on 24 October and 12 November 1809 and on 19 January 1810. But it was not until 24 July 1811 that Sarah sailed from New York on the *Drummond*.

Meanwhile, Rumford had been making arrangements for her arrival and striving to rehabilitate himself. Recovery from the traumas he had undergone was slow but he brought back some of the Aichner family to serve him and, with two helpers, he spent much time in laying out the garden. It was overlooked by a replica of Michaelangelo's large statue of Moses, which had been left behind by the Jewish banker, Monsieur Osiris, who built the house. He had intended the statue to be used as his tombstone but in the event it proved too heavy to move so he had a second one built at the cemetery.

The improvement in Rumford's health was reflected in his letters and on 24 October 1809, some four months after his divorce, he was able to write to Sarah, 'I am recovering my spirits fast. I am like one risen from the dead' and 'I have some pretty rooms prepared for you.'[20] He also found strength to immerse himself, once again, in his scientific work and his writing, and it was in this period that he did most of his work on designing lamps, calorimeters and coffee pots. He also began to take part, after an absence of four years, in the meetings at the *Institut National de France*, though it was reported that he took more notice of what he said than his audience did. He demonstrated some of his newly designed lamps and read a paper on 'The Advantage of Employing Wheels with Broad Felloes for Travelling and Pleasure Carriages'.[21] This reported that his tests had shown that it was more efficient to use wide-rimmed wheels on a vehicle both for efficiency in propelling it and in reducing the damage it did to the road surface. He was so sure that he was right that he built himself a coach with wide-rimmed wheels, but the idea did not catch on; as he drove around Paris in it still wearing – in winter – his white clothes and hat, people were more convinced than ever that he really was a cranky scientist.

He was not, however, regarded as such in Bavaria and he paid another visit to Munich, at the request of the king, in August 1810, predominantly to further advance the Academy of Arts and Sciences. Again, he felt very much at home and dined with the king on numerous occasions. He found that his English Garden was being well cared for, and forged a good relationship with Maximilian's son, Crown Prince Ludwig. But there was sad news, too. His once favourite mistress, Countess Nogarola, was dead, and Sophy, his illegitimate child by her sister, now married as Madame de Miltez, was very ill; and his aides, including Count Taxis, had been killed in battle in Russia, among 30,000 Bavarian casualties.

He left Munich on 25 October and travelled slowly back to Auteuil via Turin, Nice, Toulon, Marseilles, Montpellier, Avignon and Lyons. He got back early in December, half expecting that Sarah might have arrived from America but he had to wait another year for that. She left New York on 24 July 1811 but her journey was delayed because her ship was arrested by the British Navy as a likely blockade runner. It was taken to Plymouth where it was held for five weeks, during which time Sarah went to stay in her old home in Brompton Road and renewed her acquaintance with Sir Charles Blagden. He was unfortunately ill, but he was very anxious to help her, and she described the experience as 'a charming visit'.

Back in Plymouth she had to wait a further three weeks for a prevailing wind before crossing the Channel to Morlaix, where she had to wait another twelve days for a passport. It took a week to cover the 800 km journey to Paris, so it was 1 December when she arrived at Auteuil. Six days later she wrote to James Baldwin, Loammi's son, that she found her father's house very pleasant, that he was in excellent health, and that she 'could see nothing to prevent me from being very happy here'.[22]

She brought with her the sad news of Loammi Baldwin's death on 20 October 1807. A close friend of Rumford since the early days in Woburn, he had risen to become a distinguished engineer, and was responsible for the construction of the Middlesex Canal, linking Boston to Lowell on the Merrimack river, in 1803. But Sarah had better news for her father regarding his mother, Mrs Ruth Pierce. She was fit and well, and Rumford took the opportunity of transferring $10,000 of 3 per cent Government stock to augment her income. Not long before, he had written to her, 'My life appears to me like a dream. I have been very successful; but, on the other hand, I have been uncommonly active and enterprising. It affords me the greatest satisfaction to think that you are satisfied with the conduct of your son.'[23] The letter was signed 'your dutiful and affectionate child, Benjamin'.

Sarah and her father were both glad to see each other again after such a long interval, and she was pleased to find him so contented with his fine garden, a string of lively horses, and singing birds in the dining-room. He had, too, renewed his interest in science and he was engaged in writing an essay on 'The Nature and Effects of Order'. This was a topic that had fascinated him throughout his life and he regarded order as something akin to a deity. It was, to him, 'the necessary auxiliary of genius, the only possible instrument for securing any substantial good'.[24] The essay was intended to be an important statement of his views, but only small parts have survived and it is doubtful whether he ever completed it.

He had plenty of time for his various activities because he was becoming somewhat reclusive and had only a few regular visitors. There was Baron Delessert, his bank manager; M. Leconteux Canelux, a near neighbour; Joseph Lagrange; Mr Underwood, who had introduced him to Humphry Davy at the Royal Institution and who now lived in Paris; and Daniel Parker, a rich American also resident in Paris. He was also, considering past events, on civilized terms with his ex-wife and when she called at the house in Auteuil one day, Sarah found her very charming and thought she was an 'admirable character'.[25] She wrote: 'It was a fine match, could they but have agreed'[26] and she simply couldn't understand why they should have argued so vehemently.

There was, however, a skeleton in the cupboard in the rather mysterious shape of Victoire Lefèvre, who lived in the porter's lodge. Little is known about her, and there is some doubt about her actual name. However, that she was the last in Rumford's long line of mistresses became very obvious when she became pregnant. Sarah went off for a long stay in Switzerland to get out of the way, and Rumford's son Charles François Robert Lefèvre was born on 3 October 1813. Sarah was in no mood to celebrate the event and it did not help to stabilize her up-and-down relationship with her father. Time, however, worked wonders. When the boy grew up he joined the French army, and had a son of his own, Amédé Lefèvre, before being killed in the siege of Sevastopol during the Crimean War. Sarah, unmarried, died in 1852 when Amédé was only five years old, but it transpired that in her will she had left him $10,000 on condition that he took the name Rumford, learnt to speak English and lived some of the time in America. He took the money and changed his name but never fulfilled the other conditions.

Five weeks after Charles's birth, Mr Underwood brought Humphry Davy and his wife, together with Michael Faraday, who were touring in France, to dine with Rumford at Auteuil. It was thirteen years since Davy had first met Rumford, and he was now internationally acclaimed and at the height of his career. Rumford, by comparison, was at the end of his and leading a more and more secluded life – he used to play billiards with himself in the evenings – with the world around him falling apart because Napoleon's empire was crumbling. His grand army of 600,000 men, with contingents from Austria, Bavaria and Prussia, had marched against Russia and entered Moscow on 14 September 1812 but, forced into a fearful retreat, Napoleon lost most of his men. His armies also suffered very heavy defeats at the hands of Viscount Wellington in the Peninsular War between 1808 and 1814. In 1812 and 1813 he had in fact lost 750,000 men by death, wounding or capture. And worse was to come because, on 31 March 1814 Czar Alexander's army, with the support of many other European states who had turned against France, marched into Paris. Napoleon abdicated and was exiled to Elba; he was replaced by King Louis XVIII.

When the Russian army first began to threaten Paris, Sarah moved to Le Havre to stay with a friend, and she was still there when her father suddenly died on 21 August 1814 at the age of sixty-one. He appeared to have been in good health but he was stricken with a nervous fever and died within a few hours. The funeral, which took place in the cemetery at Auteuil three days later, was a lonely affair with only a handful of people at the graveside. M. Benjamin Delessert gave an address, but neither Sarah nor Rumford's ex-wife were present to hear his tribute – 'In England, in France, in Germany, in all parts of the continent, the people are enjoying the blessings of his discoveries; and, from the humble dwellings of the poor even to the palaces of sovereigns, all will remember that his sole aim was to be always useful to his fellow men.'[27]

Rumford's grave is covered by a horizontal marble slab and there is a vertical marble monument. The slab was originally inscribed as follows:

En Bavière

Lieutenant-Général,

Chef de l'État – Major Général,

Conseiller d'Etat,

Ministre de la Guerre.

En France

Membre de l'Institut

Académie des Sciences

but the writing is illegible today. The inscription on the monument is also very faint but it reads

À la Mémoire de
BENJAMIN THOMPSON
COMTE DE RUMFORD
né en 1753
à Woburn près Boston en Amérique
Mort le 21 Août 1814
à Auteuil

Physicien célèbre. Philanthrope éclairé
ses découvertes sur la lumière et la chaleur
ont illustré son nom. Ses travaux pour améliorer
le sort des pauvres le feront toujours chérir
désormais de l'humanité

There is a further plaque at the base of the monument, recording that the grave was restored by Harvard University and the American Academy of Arts and Sciences in 1876 after it had been damaged by a shell during the insurrection in May 1871 and again in 1923.

In his will, made in 1812, Rumford left Sarah an annuity of $400 and provided generously for Victoire Lefèvre; he bequeathed his gold watch to Davy, an enamelled snuff-box to Delessert, and a gold-headed cane to Daniel Parker; and he left all his books, plans and designs relating to military affairs to the Government of the United States for use in any military academy that might be opened. But Harvard College was the main beneficiary, with an annuity of $1,000 and the residue of the estate left for the purpose of founding a Rumford professorship 'to teach by regular courses of academical and public lectures, accompanied with proper experiments, the utility of the physical and mathematical sciences for the improvement of the useful arts, and for the extension of the industry, prosperity, happiness and well-being of Society'.[28] Such aims closely reflect those of the Royal Institution and the post is still in being today.

Sarah was at a loose end after her father's death. She stayed on at Auteuil until May 1815 but thereafter spent her time in England in the old family home at Brompton Road, in Paris and in America. Sir Charles Blagden acted as her confidant until he died in Paris in 1820, and she also remained on friendly terms with Rumford's ex-wife until her death in 1836. Sarah died on 2 December 1852 in her seventy-ninth year at Concord, in the very room in which she had been born. As her half-brother Paul Rolfe had died without children in 1819, she was the sole owner of the property, and in her will she left money for the house and estate to be converted into the Rolfe and Rumford Asylum for the poor and needy, particularly for young motherless girls. This was the culmination of a scheme hatched fifty-four years earlier by Sarah and her father in Munich, and it lasted for more than a century before it was knocked down to be replaced by an eight-lane superhighway.

FINAL VERDICT

W hat a life? What a man? What achievements? It is not surprising that Rumford's record attracted many accolades both during his life and after his death. The English poet Samuel Taylor Coleridge, who had himself given lectures at the Royal Institution, and had attended those given by Davy 'to increase his stock of metaphors',[1] paid tribute by referring to Rumford in 1796 as the reincarnation of John Howard (1726–90), the great prison reformer and founder of the Howard League for Prison Reform, with 'his zeal the same, his genius superior, his sphere of action more enlarged'. He added a sonnet:

> These, Virtue, are thy triumphs, that adorn
> Fitliest our nature, and bespeak us born
> For loftiest action; not to gaze and run
> From clime to clime; or batten in the sun,
> Dragging a drony flight from flower to flower,
> Like summer insects in a gaudy hour;
> Nor yet o'er love-sick tales with fancy rage
> And cry, ''Tis pitiful, 'tis passing strange!'
> But on life's varied views to look around
> And raise expiring sorrow from the ground;
> And he, who thus hath borne his part assign'd

In the sad fellowship of human kind,
Or for a moment soothed the bitter pain
Of a poor brother – has not lived in vain![2]

A French contemporary, Georges Cuvier, sometimes referred to as the father of comparative anatomy and palaeontology, concluded Rumford's eulogy, before the *Institut National* on 9 January 1815, with the words 'by the happy choice of his subjects as well as his works he had earned for himself both the esteem of the wise and the gratitude of the unfortunate'.[3] His obituary in the English journal the *Monthly Magazine or British Register* in May 1815, described him as 'an honour to the whole human race'.[4] Above all, F.D. Roosevelt rated him, along with Benjamin Franklin and Thomas Jefferson, as 'the greatest mind America has produced'.[5]

Yet he died and was buried almost alone, and very few people today know who he was or anything about what he did. Why? The generally accepted view is that it was because he was an insufferable genius who treated the people with whom he had to work with such disdain and contempt that he simply made more and more enemies as he grew older. One commentator wrote 'he was utterly devoid of humour and humanism; hard, brittle, self-centred from first to last'.[6] Another wrote 'he was unbelievably cold-blooded, inherently egotistic and a snob',[7] and another 'he was the most unpleasant personality in the history of science since Isaac Newton'.[8]

Even his own daughter judged that 'he was fond of having his own way, even, as I fancied, to despite me'[9] and that:

'He could go one way or the other. And it was invariably the case, that when quiet and happy himself, he was like others, or, in other words, agreeable; but when perplexed with cares or business, or much occupied, there was no living with him.'[10] Cuvier himself commented that 'it must be confessed that he exhibited in conversation and intercourse, and in all his demeanour, a feeling which would seem most extraordinary in a man who was always so well treated by others, and who himself had done so much good to others. It was as if while he had been rendering all these services to his fellow-men he had no real love or regard for them. It would appear as if the vile passions which he had observed in the miserable objects committed to his care, or those other passions, not less vile, which his success and fame had excited among his rivals, had embittered him towards human nature.'[11] And the *Monthly Magazine or British Register* obituary reported that at the Royal Institution 'the Count conducted himself with such a degree of *hauteur* which disgusted its patrons, and almost broke the heart of our amiable friend and its first professor, Dr Garnett'.[12]

The oddity, however, is that this egocentric aspect of Rumford's personality was completely at variance with so many of his deeds. For there can be no doubt that he sincerely used his technical expertise and his original ideas of social reform both to advance scientific knowledge and to do good works. 'My purpose,' he wrote, 'is to increase the enjoyment and comforts of life, especially in the lower and more numerous classes of society.'[13] And 'my greatest delight arises from the silent contemplation of having succeeded in schemes and labors for the benefit of mankind'.[14] It wasn't, then, what he did that was at fault, because he was in many ways a social reformer well ahead of his times. It was rather the way in which he did it that was responsible for his unpopularity and which demonstrated the split personality of his complex character. The humanitarian, caring, thoughtful and philanthropic side of his nature, exemplified in his phrase 'we must make benevolence more fashionable',[15] was dwarfed by meaner streaks described by such adjectives as self-satisfied, know-all, insufferable, single-minded, acerbic, opportunistic, over-bearing, superior, vain, truculent and self-important.

One commentator tried to summarize it when he wrote: 'although Rumford disliked people to his dying day, as much as they disliked him, he loved humanity'.[16] That seems to involve some contradiction in terms, but emphasizes the extraordinary and enigmatic nature of the man. As does his own self-assessment, written in his last letter to his former patron, the dying Lord Sackville: 'No man supported a better moral character than I do and no man is better satisfied with himself.'[17] Not many people could ever bring themselves to write such a sentence.

APPENDICES

1. The first page of Rumford's spy letter

The original letter, without the words in invisible ink, read as follows:

Sir,

> **If you will be so kind as to deliver to**

.... of Boston the papers which I

left in your care and take his Receipt for the same,

you will much oblige.

> **Your humble servant**

Saturday May 6th 1775.

When the words in invisible ink (printed here in italic) were developed, it read as follows:

Woburn May 6th 1775

Sir, In compliance with your desires I embrace this *first opportunity that has offered since I left* **Sir**, *Boston to send you some account of the* *situation of affairs in this part of the Country.*

If you will be so kind as to deliver to *I need not trouble you with a particular account* **............................ of Boston the papers which I** *of the affairs at Concord on Wednesday, May 19th . . .* **left in your care and take his Receipt for the same,** *nor of this subsequent gathering at Cambridge . . . as* **you will much oblige.** *you have doubtless already* *better intelligence of these affairs than I am able* *to give you.* **Your humble servant**

The only information that I can give you *that can be of any consequence . . . . received* **Saturday May 6th 1775** *from a Field Officer in the* *Rebel Army (if that mass of confusion may be called* *an Army) & from a member of the Provincial* *Congress that is now sitting at Watertown.* *By them I learn that an Army consisting of* *30,000 effective men is speedily to be raised in* *the four New England Governments, & that the* *quota for this Province is 13600. That as soon* *as this Army shall be raised & regulated it is* *generally supposed that the first movement* *will be to make a feint attack upon the Town* *of Boston, & at the same time to attempt the* *Castle with the main body of the Army . . .*

2. The first page of Rumford's 'Miscellanius Observations upon the State of the Rebel Army'

Upon Sunday October 15th I saw 16 *flat-bottom'd* boats or *Batteaus* lying just below Cambridge Bridge, & two more were making in the yard ----- The workmen informed me that one was finished every day, and that more workmen were daily expected from Newbury. – These boats are built of common deal Boards, & in general will contain from 50 to 60 men, including the Rowers. -- What number of them were to be made I could not learn.

It is generally supposed in the Rebel Army that an attack is designed upon either Charleston or Boston, or both ---- and that the boats are preparing to transport Troops to these places. But many of the more intelligent and among them some of their principal Officers rather suppose those preparations are only to amuse Ye Kings Troops, and by keeping them continually alarm'd with apprehension of being attacked prevent their going to distant parts of the Country to Ravage.

About the 13th October a return was made of the number of Men, that all the boats of every denomination (exclusive of the flat-bottom'd boats) in the Rebel Camp, were capable of transporting --- and I was told by a Person who saw said return that the total number was 550.

From the best information I have been able to get with respect to their *Military Stores*, the total quantity of *Gun-Powder* that they have in their Camp (exclusive

of

3. Rumford's Essays

1. 'An Account of an Establishment for the Poor at Munich' (1796)
2. 'Of the Fundamental Principles on which General Establishments for the Relief of the Poor may be Formed in all Countries' (1797)
3. 'Of Food; and Particularly of Feeding the Poor' (1796)
4. 'Of Chimney Fire-places, with Proposals for Improving them to Save Fuel; to Render Dwelling Houses more Comfortable and Salubrious and Effectively to Prevent Chimneys from Smoking' (1796)
5. 'A Short Account of Several Public Institutions Lately Formed in Bavaria' (1797)
6. 'Of the Management of Fire and the Economy of Fuel' (1797)
7. 'Of the Manner in which Heat is Propagated in Fluids' (1797)
8. 'Of the Propagation of Heat in Various Substances' (1798)
9. 'An Experimental Inquiry Concerning the Source of Heat Which is Excited by Friction' (1798)
10. 'On the Construction of Kitchen Fire-places and Kitchen Utensils; together with Remarks and Observations Relating to the Various Processes of Cookery and Proposals for Improving that Most Useful Art' – in 3 parts – (1799–1800)
11. 'Observations Concerning Chimney Fireplaces' (1796)
12. 'Of the Salubrity of Warm Rooms' (1804)

13. 'The Salubrity of Warm Bathing and the Principles on Which Warm Baths should be Constructed' (1804)
14. 'Supplementary Observations Relating to the Management of Fires in Closed Fireplaces' (1804)
15. 'Of the Use of Steam as a Vehicle for Transporting Heat from One Place to Another' (1804)
16. 'Of the Management of Light in Illumination' (1812)
17. 'An Enquiry Concerning the Source of the Light which is Manifested in the Combustion of Inflammable Bodies' (1812)
18. 'Of the Excellent Qualities of Coffee and the Art of Making it in the Highest Perfection' (1812)

NOTES

Where a short title is provided, details are given in the bibliography.

1. An Eye for the Main Chance

1. Ellis, p. 7.
2. Ibid., p. 8.
3. Brown, *Benjamin Thompson, Count Rumford*, p. 1.
4. Ellis, p. 8.
5. Ibid., p. 15.
6. *Silliman's American Journal of Science*, vol. 33 (1838), p. 21.
7. Ellis, p. 43.
8. Ibid., p. 7.
9. Brown, *Count Rumford; Physicist Extraordinary*, p. 7.
10. Ellis, p. 22.
11. Rumford, *Complete Works*, vol. I, p. 98.
12. *Chalmer's Biographical Dictionary*, vol. 29, p. 298.
13. Ellis, p. 44.
14. Johnson, p. 116.
15. Ibid.
16. Sparrow, p. 39.
17. Clark, p. 12.
18. Ibid., p. 14.
19. Ellis, p. 65.
20. Ibid., pp. 67–8.
21. Ibid., p. 68.
22. Sparrow, p. 36.
23. Ibid., p. 281.
24. Ibid., p. 279.

2. Fortunes of War

1. Boswell, vol. ii, p. 412.
2. Thackeray, J.M. The author does not know the source of this and would appreciate any information.
3. Chambers, p. 1559.
4. Brown, *Benjamin Thompson, Count Rumford*, p. 47.
5. Ibid.
6. Ellis, p. 116.
7. Rumford, *Complete Works*, vol. I, p. 98.
8. Well, C.R., *History of the Royal Society*, vol. II, p. 212.
9. Ellis, p. 109.

10. Brown, *Benjamin Thompson, Count Rumford*, p. 61.
11. Ibid., p. 325.
12. Brown, *Count Rumford, Physicist Extraordinary*, p. 31.
13. Parkinson, p. 110.
14. Sparrow, p. 60.
15. Ibid.
16. Brown, *Benjamin Thompson, Count Rumford*, p. 88.

3. Bavarian Adventure

1. Brown, *Benjamin Thompson, Count Rumford*, p. 93.
2. Ellis, p. 157.
3. Ibid.
4. Brown, *Benjamin Thompson, Count Rumford*, p. 90.
5. Larsen, p. 47.
6. Ibid., pp. 52–3.
7. Rumford, *Complete Works*, vol. IV, p. 233.
8. Ibid., p. 242.
9. Sparrow, p. 87.
10. Ellis, p. 196.
11. Ibid., p. 197.
12. *The Oxford Dictionary of Quotations* (OUP, 1964), p. 412.
13. Ellis, p. 662.
14. Brown, *Benjamin Thompson, Count Rumford*, p. 147.
15. Ibid., p. 146.
16. Sparrow, p. 106.

4. The Countess

1. Brown, *Benjamin Thompson, Count Rumford*, p. 165.
2. Ellis, p. 224.
3. Ibid., p. 223.
4. Ibid., p. 222.
5. Ibid., p. 225.
6. Ibid., p. 212.
7. Ibid.
8. Brown, *Benjamin Thompson, Count Rumford*, p. 167.
9. Larsen, p. 77.
10. Ellis, p. 209.
11. Ibid., p. 212.
12. Ellis, p. 242.
13. Rumford, *Complete Works*, vol. I, p. 472.
14. Ellis, p. 281.
15. Ibid., p. 318.
16. Ibid., p. 319.

5. The Nature of Heat

1. Rumford, *Complete Works*, vol. II, p. 188.
2. Brown, *Benjamin Thompson, Count Rumford*, p. 183.
3. Moore, W.J., *Physical Chemistry* (Longmans, 1968), p. 213.
4. Sparrow, pp. 216–17.
5. Tyndall, p. 36.
6. Sparrow, p. 222.

7. Peacock, T.L., *Headlong Hall* (Everyman's Library, Dent, 1910), p. 2.
8. Brown, *Benjamin Thompson, Count Rumford*, p. 195.
9. Rumford, *Complete Works*, vol. I, p. 472.
10. Brown, *Benjamin Thompson, Count Rumford*, p. 255.
11. Rumford, *Complete Works*, vol. I, p. 482.
12. Ibid., p. 483.
13. Ibid., p. 490.
14. Tyndall, p. 72.
15. Sparrow, p. 223.
16. Rumford, *Complete Works*, vol. II, p. 16.
17. Lenard, p. 283.
18. Tyndall, p. 46.

6. *The Ingenious Inventor*

1. Rumford, *Complete Works*, vol. IV, p. 3.
2. Ibid., p. 134.
3. Brown, *Benjamin Thompson, Count Rumford*, p. 302.
4. Brown, *The Collected Works of Count Rumford*, vol. IV, p. 97.
5. Rumford, *Complete Works*, vol. II, p. 484.
6. Ibid., p. 542.
7. Ibid., p. 543.
8. Ibid., vol. III, p. 6.
9. Ibid., vol. II, p. 566.
10. Brown, *Benjamin Thompson, Count Rumford*, p. 235.
11. Rumford, *Complete Works*, vol. IV, p. 407.
12. Ibid., vol. III, p. 198.
13. Ibid., vol. IV, p. 476.
14. Ibid., p. 618.
15. Ibid., p. 654.
16. Ibid., p. 617.
17. Ibid., p. 411.
18. Ellis, p. 536.
19. Ibid., pp. 506–7.
20. *Blackwood's Magazine*, vol. XIV, December 1823.

7. *The Royal Institution*

1. Ellis, p. 336.
2. Ibid., p. 343.
3. Ibid., p. 344.
4. Ibid., p. 290.
5. Ibid., p. 353.
6. Ibid., p. 355.
7. Larsen, p. 114.
8. Bence Jones, p. 44.
9. Ibid., p. 46.
10. Webb, S. and B., *English Local Government; English Poor Law History; Part 1, 'The Old Poor Law'* (London, 1927), p. 170.
11. Bence Jones, p. 47.
12. Ellis, p. 384.

13. Sparrow, p. 108.
14. Ibid., p. 107.
15. Ellis, p. 381.
16. Ibid., p. 380.
17. Ibid., p. 390.
18. Ibid.
19. Ibid., p. 391.
20. Ibid., p. 363.
21. Brown, *Benjamin Thompson, Count Rumford*, p. 221.
22. Rumford, *Complete Works*, vol. IV, pp. 771–85.
23. Brown, *Benjamin Thompson, Count Rumford*, p. 225.
24. Bence Jones, p. 144.
25. Brown, *Benjamin Thompson, Count Rumford*, p. 213.
26. Paris, p. 90.
27. Sparrow, p. 125.
28. Brown, *Benjamin Thompson, Count Rumford*, p. 244.
29. Ibid., p. 247.
30. Ibid.
31. Ibid., p. 248.

8. A Female Dragon

1. Rumford, *Complete Works*, vol. II, pp. 23–131.
2. Ibid., pp. 166–88.
3. Larsen, p. 186.
4. Thorpe, p. 89.
5. Ibid.
6. Ibid., p. 90.
7. Ibid., pp. 89–90.
8. Sparrow, p. 160.
9. Ellis, p. 542.
10. Ibid., p. 548.
11. Ibid.
12. Ibid., p. 551.
13. Ibid., p. 559.
14. Ibid., p. 560.
15. Ibid.
16. Ibid., p. 562.
17. Ibid., p. 564.
18. Ibid.
19. Ibid., p. 562.
20. Ibid., p. 567.
21. Rumford, *Complete Works*, vol. III, p. 461.
22. Ellis, p. 595.
23. Ibid., pp. 599–600.
24. Ibid., p. 620.
25. Ibid., p. 602.
26. Ibid.
27. Ibid., p. 615.
28. Ibid., p. 635.

9. Final Verdict

1. Paris, vol. 1, p. 138.
2. *The Watchman* (Bristol, 1796), no. 5, p. 140.
3. Ellis, p. 621.
4. Ibid., p. 622.
5. Quoted in *Concise Dictionary of Scientists* (W. & R. Chambers, 1989), p. 335.

6. Thompson, J.A., quoted by Adams, C. Raymond, 'Benjamin Thompson, Count Rumford', *Scientific Monthly*, 1950, 71, p. 381.

7. Sparrow, p. 259.

8. Brush, Stephen G., 'Marvelous bedtime reading for physicists', *Physics Today*, November 1979, p. 55.

9. Larsen, p. 91.

10. Bence Jones, p. 60.

11. Ellis, p. 619.

12. Ibid., p. 622.

13. Ibid., p. 245.

14. Bence Jones, p. 71.

15. Ellis, p. 384.

16. Salzer, O.T., *American Journal of Education*, vol. 61, no. 9, September 1984, p. 795.

17. Sparrow, p. 78.

BIBLIOGRAPHY

Books

Berman, Morris, *Social Change and Scientific Organization: The Royal Institution, 1799–1844* (The Royal Institution, London, 1978)

Boswell, James, *The Life of Dr. Johnson*, vol. 11 (Privately printed for the Navarre Society, London, 1924)

Brown, Sanborn C., *Count Rumford; Physicist Extraordinary* (Heinemann, 1964)

Brown, Sanborn C. (ed.) *The Collected Works of Count Rumford* (vols I–V) (Harvard, 1970–1)

Brown, Sanborn C., *Benjamin Thompson, Count Rumford* (MIT Press, Cambridge, MA, 1979)

Caroe, A.D.R., *The House of the Royal Institution* (The Royal Institution, London, 1963)

Clark, Philip, *American War of Independence* (Chivers Press, 1988)

Chambers Biographical Dictionary (ed.) Magnus Magnusson (Chambers, 1990)

Cost, March, *The Countess* (Cassell, 1963)

Dwight, C. Harrison, *Sir Benjamin Thompson, Count Rumford* (Privately printed in Cincinnati, 1960)

Ellis, George E., *Memoir of Sir Benjamin Thompson, Count Rumford with Notices of his Daughter* (American Academy of Arts and Sciences, Boston, 1871)

Fischer, David Hackett, *Paul Revere's Ride* (Oxford University Press, 1994)

Hale, R.W., *Some Account of Benjamin Thompson* (Addison C. Getchell & Son, Boston, 1927)

Hill, Douglas, *Georgian London* (Macdonald & Co., 1970)

Houey, Erica, *The American Revolution* (Dryad Press Limited, 1986)

Jones, Dr Bence, *The Royal Institution; Its Founder and its First Professors* (Longmans, Green & Co., 1871)

Johnson, Paul, *A History of the American People* (Weidenfeld & Nicholson, 1997)

Bibliography

Larsen, Egon, *An American in Europe. The Life of Benjamin Thompson, Count Rumford* (Rider & Co., New York, 1953)

Lenard, Philipp, *Great Men of Science* (G. Bell & Sons Ltd, 1954)

Martin, Thomas, *The Royal Institution* (The Royal Institution, London, 1961)

Paris, J.A., *The Life of Sir Humphry Davy* (Henry Colburn & Richard Bentley, 1831)

Parkinson, Roger, *The American Revolution* (Wayland Publishers, 1971)

Pictet, A. (ed.) *Bibliothèque Britannique, Science et Arts, vol. XVII et al.* (Geneva, 1802)

Porter, Roy, *London: A Social History* (Hamish Hamilton, 1994)

Rudé, George, *Hanoverian London 1714–1808* (Secker & Warburg, 1971)

Rumford, Benjamin, Count of, *Philosophical Papers* (T. Cadell, Jun. & W. Davies, vol. i, 1802)

Rumford, Count, The Complete Works (The American Academy of Arts and Sciences, 4 vols, 1870–73)

Sparrow, W.J., *Knight of the White Eagle. A Bibliography of Sir Benjamin Thompson, Count Rumford* (Hutchinson, 1964)

Thompson, James Alden, *Count Rumford of Massachusetts* (Farrar & Rinehart, New York, 1935)

Tyndall, John, *Heat: A Mode of Motion* (Longmans, Green & Co., 1880)

Articles

Adams, C. Raymond, 'Benjamin Thompson, Count Rumford' (*Science Monthly*, 71, December 1950, p. 380)

Brown, S.C., 'Count Rumford and the Caloric Theory of Heat' (*Proceedings of the American Philosophical Society*, vol. 93, no. 4, September 1949, p. 316)

Brown, S.C., 'Rumford Lamps' (*Proceedings of the American Philosophical Society*, vol. 96, no. 1, February 1952, p. 37)

Brown, S.C., 'Count Rumford's Concept of Heat' (*American Journal of Physics*, vol. 20, 1952, p. 331)

Brown, S.C. and Scott, K., 'Count Rumford, International Informer' (*New England Quarterly*, 21 March 1984, p. 34)

Cummings, A.D., 'The Eighteenth Century's Fuel Efficiency Expert' (*Discovery*, 8, April–May 1947, p. 120)

Bibliography

Day, Peter, '"Mr. Secretary, Colonel, Admiral, Philosopher Thompson"; the European odyssey of Count Rumford' (*European Review*, vol. 3, no. 2, 1995, pp. 103–11)

Lewellen, J., 'Count Rumford, Theorist of Heat' (*Science Digest*, 39, February 1956, p. 86)

Maechling, C., 'Count Rumford: Scientific Adventurer' (*History Today*, 22, April 1972, p. 245)

Martin, Thomas, 'Origins of the Royal Institution' (*British Journal for the History of Science*, I, 1962, pp. 49–63)

Mendoza, E., 'The historical approach to the mechanical equivalent of heat' (*School Science Review*, 44, p. 11)

Mitchell, Wilson, 'Count Rumford' (*Scientific American*, 203–4, October 1960, p. 158)

Sparrow, W.J., 'Count Rumford as a Spy' (*Annals of Science*, 11, 1955, pp. 320–30)

Sparrow, W.J., 'Rumford's Photometer' (*School Science Review*, 134, November 1956, pp. 43–7)

William, W. Mattieu, 'On Rumford's Scientific Discoveries' (*Proceedings of the Royal Institution*, vi, 24 March 1871, p. 227)

INDEX

aether, the, 140
Aichner, the family, 63, 146, 147
Albemarle Street, 121
American Academy of Arts and
    Sciences, 66
American Military Academy, 116
Amiens, Treaty of, 140
Anderson's Institution, 122
Anymeetle, 63
Appleton, John, 4
Apreece, Mrs, 135
Argand, Ami, 95
Argand lamps, 95
Aristotle, 100
Ashley's Riding School, 63
Au, 49
Augusta, Princess, 51
Auteuil, 149, 156

Bacon, Francis, 78
Baldwin, James, 61, 152
Baldwin, Loammi, 5, 61, 65, 74, 115,
    152
Ball, Revd, 25
Banks, Sir Joseph, 27, 121, 133
Barnard, Revd Thomas, 5
Baumgarten, Countess, 42, 73
Baumgarten, Sophy, 42, 131, 152

Bavaria, 40
Bayern, 40
Beddoes, Thomas, 128
begging in Bavaria, 48
Belderbusch, Count, 43
Bernard, Thomas, 117, 125, 133
Berthollet, Claude, 79, 132
Berzelius, Johann, 79
Black, Joseph, 79, 82
Blagden, Sir Charles, 56, 122, 137,
    149, 152, 158
Blanchard, François, 24
Boerhaave, Hermann, 77
Bolingbroke, Lady, 57
Bordier, 99
Boston, 11–16
    massacre, 11
    'tea party', 11
Boulton, Matthew, 96, 127
Bourghausen, General, 39
Boyle, Robert, 79
Bragg, Laurence, 136
Bragg, William, 36
Breed's Hill, 13
Bretzenheim, Count von, 39
British Register, 160
British Thermal Unit (BThU), 82
Brompton Road, 117

Brompton Row, 117
Brown, Prof. Sanford C., viii, 17
Bunker Hill, 13
Burke, Edmund, 21
Byfield, 3

Cadell, T., 64, 133
caloric theory, 79
calorie, the, 82
calorimeter, 105
Cambridge, 5
candela unit, 98
Canelax, M. Leconteux, 154
cannon boring, 83–7
Cape Cod, 1
Capen, Hopestill, 4
carbon monoxide, 128
Carleton, General, 22
Carron company, 104
Cavendish, Henry, 79, 129, 140
Celsius, A., 81
central heating, 104
Champlain, Lake, 13
Charleston, 62
Charleston, 30, 33
Chatham, Earl of, 10
chimneys, 100
Church, Benjamin, 16
Clausius, Rudolf, 92
Cobbett, William, 113
Coercive Act, 11
coffee, 110
Coleridge, S.T., 159
Concord, 7, 12, 74
cooking, 106

Copley medal, 47, 93
Cora, 72
Corn and Bread Bill, 106
Cornwallis, Lord, 31, 33
Cruickshank, Isaac, 102
Curwen, Samuel, 24
Cuvier, Georges, 160

Dalton, John, 79, 92
Dashwood, Francis, 21
Davies, W, 64, 133
Davy, Humphry, 79, 87, 127, 134–5, 155
de Chabann, Marquise, 63
Declaration of Independence, 35
de Kalb, Baroness Laura, 68, 71, 131
de la Motte, Francis Henry, 33
de Laplace, Marquis, 79, 149
Delessert, Baron, 154, 156
De Miltez, Madam, 152
De Staehl, Madame, 132
Deux-Ponts, Duke of, 131
Dewar, James, 136
Dorchester, 13
dumplings, 110

Einstein, Albert, 140
Elector of Bavaria, 39
Eliot, E.J., 118
Ellis, Revd G.E., viii
energy, 91–2
English Garden, Munich, 51–8
éprouvette, 26
ether, the, 140

Fahrenheit, G.D., 81
Faraday, Michael, 86, 135–6, 155
fire-places, 101
First Continental Congress, 11
Fisher, John, 33
Fort Golgotha, 35
Fort Ticonderoga, 13
Fourcroy, 132
Frank, Father Ignaz, 42, 67,
Franklin stove, 104
Franklin, Benjamin, 104, 160
Fraser, William, 38
French Revolution, 36, 55

Gage, Thomas, 12, 14
Gainsborough, Thomas, 19, 38
Galileo, 81
gallotanic acid, 17
Garnett, Thomas, 122, 125, 127, 161
George III, 15, 21
Georgia, 11
Georgia, Province of, 24
Germain, Lady Betty, 22
Germain, Lord George, 21, 27, 34
Gibbon, Edward, 19, 38, 74
Gilbert, William, 140
Gillray, James, 102, 125
Gott, Benjamin, 105
Greenfield, Prof. Susan, vi, 136
Grenville, Lord George, 10, 114
gunnery, 26
gunpowder, 25
gunpowder trier, 26

Hardy, Sir Charles, 27, 29

Harvard College, 5, 61, 157
Harvey, William, 140
Hay, Dr, 5, 6
heat, nature of, 77–94
Hell Fire Club, 21
Hirschanger, 51
Holy Roman Empire, 41
Hooke, Robert, 79
Howard, John, 159
Howe, General William, 15, 18
Huntingdon, 34
Hutton, Charles, 26
Huygens, Christiaan, 140

Innes, Col. Alexander, 30
Inspector General of Artillery, 116
Institut National de France, 98, 105,
     132, 145, 151
Intolerable Act, 11
invisible ink letter, 17
iron sulphate, 17
Isar, river, 51

Jefferson, Thomas, 132, 160
Jeffries, Dr John, 24
Jollien, Madame, 132
Joseph II, 39
Joule, James Prescott, 92–4
joule, the, 89
Jourdan, General, 69

Keith, Sir R.M., 38, 39
Kemble, Col. Stephen, 15
Kew Gardens, 51
Kiev, 100

Index

kilocalorie, 82

kilojoule, 89

kinetic energy, 91

kinetic theory, 78

King of Bavaria, 149

King, Rufus, 115

King's American Dragoons, 32, 34, 37

Knight of the White Eagle, 54

kreutzer, the, 119

Lagrange, Joseph, 132, 142, 154

Lambert, J.H., 96

Laplace, Madame, 132

Laplace, Marquis de, 132

La Tour, General, 68

Laurens, Henry, 31, 38

Lavoisier, Antoine, 79, 141

Lavoisier, Madame, 132, 137, 140, 143, 146

Lavoisier's list of elements, 80

Lefèvre, Amédé, 154

Lefèvre, Victoire, 154

Lefèvre, C.F.R., 154

Leibniz, Gottfried, 79

Leopold II, 54

Leslie, John, 79

Lexington, 12

lighting, 95

Lloyd's Neck, 34

Locke, John, 78

London, 19–20

Longfellow, 12

Louis XVI, 55

Louis XVIII, 155

Lowell, 153

Luckington, Mrs, 63

Ludwig, Crown Prince, 151

Mainz, 42

Marble Arch, 20

Marie Antoinette, 35

Massachusetts, 1

Massachusetts Spy, The, 15

Mathias, Thomas, J., 58

Maximilian III, 42

Maximilian Joseph, 131

Maximilian of Zweibrücken, Prince, 38

Mayer, J.R., 90–3

Mayflower, The, 1

mechanical equivalent of heat, 89

Medford, 3

Medical Pneumatic Institution, 128

Medmenham Abbey, 21

Mer de Glace, 143

Merrimack, River, 153

Mezhirich, 100

Michaelangelo, 150

Monthly Magazine, 160

Morawitzky, Count, 68

Moreau, General, 69

Moses, statue of, 150

Munich, 41, 68

City Council, 53, 75

Murray, Captain David, 32, 37

Narragansett Bay, 15

New Hampshire, 7, 9

New Plymouth, 1

Newton, Isaac, 160
nitrous oxide, 128
Nogarola, Countess, 42, 56, 67, 152
North, Lord, 10, 21, 34
nutrition, 106

order, 153
Osiris, Monsieur, 150

Palatinate, 41
Pallebot, 99
Palmerston, Lady, 57, 60, 122
Paris, J.A., 129
Paris, Treaty of, 35
Parker, Daniel, 154
passage thermometer, 46
Paulze, Marie-Anne-Pierrette, 141
Pennsylvania stove, 104
People's Committee, 14
Percy, Revd Ebenzer, 35
Philadelphia, 11, 12
photometer, 96
Pictet, Prof. M.A., 2, 71, 117, 123,
        143
Pierce, Col. Benjamin, 8
Pierce, Josiah, 2
Pierce, Mrs Ruth, 153
Pierce, Paul, 8
Pilgrim Fathers, 1
Pindar, Peter, 102, 124
Pitt, William, 10
Poggendorff, Johann, 92
Porter, George, 136
potato, 109
potential energy, 109

Potter, Thomas, 21
Priestley, Joseph, 140
Principles of Gunnery, 26
Prout, William, 47

Queen's Rangers, 34
Quinquet lamp, 96

Red Deer Grassy Plains, 51
Revere, Paul, 12
Risbeck, Kaspar, 43
Robins, Benjamin, 26
Rockingham, Marquis of, 21, 34
Rolfe and Rumford Asylum, 158
Rolfe, Paul, 158
Romford, 7
Roosevelt, F.D., 160
Rosetta Stone, 130
Ross, Admiral John, 29
Rousseau, 55
Royal Institution, 124–36
Royal Society, 27, 47, 66
Rumford, Count, see Benjamin
        Thompson,
    essays, list of, 168
    illuminators, 98
    lamps, 98
    medals, 66
    roaster, 107
    soup, 111
Rumford, Countess, 69, 115
Rumfordstrasse, 69

Sackville, Lord, 22, 34, 162
St Paul's Cathedral, 60

Salem, 4, 11
samp, 112
Sandwich, Earl of, 29
Saxony, 41
Scarborough, 42
Schwabinger Gasse, 42
Second Continental Congress, 12
Secretary for the Province of
    Georgia, 24
Sheffield, Lord, 63
silk, 30
SI units, 93
Snow, Mrs, 62
soup kitchens, 112
soups, 110
Sparrow, W.J., viii
specific heat capacity, 82
Spreti, Lt, 70
Stacey, Mr, 61
Stamp Act, 11
steam heating, 104
Stein, Mr Elbridge W., 7
Stoneland Lodge, 23, 25

Taxis, Captain Count, 70, 72, 115,
    152
Taxis, Princess, 71
Thackeray, 20
Theodore, Carl, 39, 44, 57, 67, 75,
    131
thermometers, 46, 81
thermoscope, 138
Thompson Island, 40
Thompson, Benjamin,
    apprenticeships, 4

background, 1–9
birth, 1
burial, 157
final verdict, 159–62
first marriage, 8
handwriting, 16–18
knighthood, 39
leaves Boston, 15
major's commission, 9
notebook, 4
schooling, 3
second marriage, 145
spying, 16–18
tombstone, 156
Thompson, Hiram, 2, 3
Thompson, Sarah, 9, 60–76, 115,
    150–8
Tower of London, 31
Tübingen, 90
Tyburn Hill, 20
Tyndall, John, 86, 94, 136

Underwood, Mr, 128, 154, 155
United States, Recognition of, 36

Volta, Count Alessandro, 56, 132
voltaic pile, 46
von Helmholtz, Hermann, 92
von Sckell, Friedrich Ludwig, 52

Walker, Revd Timothy, 7
Walpole, Thomas, 40
War of Independence, 9–18
Washington, George, 12, 33
Watt, James, 96, 127

Webster, Lady Elizabeth, 57
Webster, Thomas, 122, 134
Wellington, Viscount, 155
Wentworth, John, 9, 16, 22, 40
Wilberforce, William, 106, 118
Wilkes, John, 20
Willard, Dr Joseph, 61
William L. Clements Library, 16
Winthrop, John, 2

Withyam, 25
Woburn, 1
Wolcot, Dr John, 102
workhouses, 49

Yorktown, 33
Young, Thomas, 79, 130

Zweibrücken, Duke of, 55, 57, 67